MASSIMILIANO AFIERO

SS-KAMPFGRUPPE PEIPER

1943–1945

KAGERO

MASSIMILIANO AFIERO

SS-KAMPFGRUPPE PEIPER

1943–1945

First Edition
© by KAGERO Publishing

AUTHOR
Massimiliano Afiero

PHOTO CREDITS
Bundesarchiv, Germany (BA); Washington, D.C., National Archives and Records Administration (NARA); Berlin Document Center (BDC); Istituto di Storia Moderna, Lubljana (MZNS);
Deutsche Wochenschau (DW); ECPA; Nation Europa Verlag, Coburg (NEV); HTM Budapest
Imperial War Museum (IWM); Munin Velag
Private collections: Massimo Antigoni, Michael Cremin, Martin Månsson, Günther Scappini,
Horst Schumann, Pierre Tiquet, Charles Trang, Herbert Walther, Studio Fotografico Croce (Maurizio Cavalloni)
N.B. The author declares himself to be fully responsible to settle any fees for those images for which it has not been possible to determine the source and to correct any errors or omissions in subsequent editions.

COLOUR PROFILES
Jacek Pasieczny, Arkadiusz Wróbel

TRANSLATION/PROOFREADING
Ralph Riccio

DTP
KAGERO STUDIO

LUBLIN 2018
All rights reserved.
No part of this publication may be used in print media or radio and television broadcasts without prior written permission from the Publisher

ISBN 978-83-951575-0-9

KAGERO Publishing
Akacjowa 100, os. Borek, Turka
20-258 Lublin 62, Poland
phone/fax +48 81 501-21-05
e-mail: kagero@kagero.pl, marketing@kagero.pl
www.kagero.pl, shop.kagero.pl

Table of contents

JOACHIM PEIPER 9

AT WAR 11

UKRAINE, FEBRUARY-MARCH 1943 13

OPERATION "ZITADELLE" 24

TRANSFER TO ITALY 28

UKRAINIAN FRONT 1943-44 32

ON THE NORMANDY FRONT 45

THE ARDENNES OFFENSIVE 53

THE HUNGARIAN FRONT 80

FINAL COMBAT IN AUSTRIA 99

JOACHIM PEIPER SERVICE RECORD DATA 105

LIST OF AWARDS AND PROMOTIONS 106

BIBLIOGRAPHY 108

SS-Kampfgruppe Peiper 1943-1945

Joachim "Jochen" Peiper, one of the most famous and valorous German officers to serve in the Waffen-SS, but is also a person who is normally described in official histories as a monster, as one of the most ferocious German war criminals of the Second World War. It is always very difficult to speak of Peiper the soldier, even when wishing to examine the subject only from a strictly military-historical point of view. The intent of this book is mainly to trace the military career of Jochen Peiper and to describe the military actions in which the units of the *Leibstandarte Adolf Hitler* that he commanded were involved, actions which to this day are still studied and analyzed in all of the world's military academies and to which new studies and historical military publications are devoted. Those actions were carried out by courageous and fearless men, led in battle by worthy commanders, not by fanatic bloodthirsty criminals. There were undoubtedly abuses, crimes against enemy prisoners and against civilians, all the inevitable consequences of war, of clashes between enemy units carried out behind urban areas, and we say all of this without wishing to even minimally justify or glorify these abhorrent actions. Beginning in 1943, Peiper was always assigned to command of motorized and armored units of the *Leibstandarte Adolf Hitler*, first during the fighting on the Kharkov front between February and March 1943, as commander of III.(gep.)/2, then moving on to the fighting on the Kursk front, the new campaign on the Ukrainian front between autumn and winter of 1943-44 as commander of *SS-Pz.Rgt.1*, the fighting on the Normandy front, the counteroffensive in the Ardennes, until the final battles in Hungary and Austria. The analysis of the various battles is told through statements by the direct participants, war reports from the period and original documents, all of which as always are accompanied by exceptional photographs, maps, documents and images drawn from military archives throughout the world and from major private collections, all to render the subject matter as interesting as possible. Hoping that I have produced a worthwhile piece of work, I would like to take this opportunity to thank all of the friends and collaborators who contributed to this book, and I invite everyone to suggest any additions or corrections.

Massimiliano Afiero

SS-Obersturmbannführer Joachim Peiper, with the Knight's Cross with Oak Leaves around his neck.

Joachim Peiper

Joachim Peiper was born in Berlin on 30 January 1915, to a middle-class family. His father, Woldemar, had been an officer in the Imperial Army and had fought in East Africa in 1904, where he was awarded the Military Cross after having been wounded a total of seven times and having been ill with malaria. When the First World War broke out, his father was recalled to service and sent to Turkey. Nevertheless, because of heart problems stemming from the after-effects of his malaria, he was retired from service in 1915. After the war, he joined the Free Corps and took part in the fighting in Silesia.

Peiper had two brothers, Hans-Hasso and Horst. Both served in the SS. Hans-Hasso, a member of an *SS-Totenkpfverbande*, died in 1942 after having tried to commit suicide, while Horst died in 1941.

After having attended primary school, Peiper moved on to the *Goethe Oberrealschule* in Berlin. However, he left it in 1933 without having completed his exams. After the war, his father said that young Joachim had decided to become a cavalry officer and thus signed up for a riding school. One day, a high-ranking SS officer who was visiting the school invited all of the students to enlist in the SS cavalry units. And thus, on 12 October 1933, Peiper became a member of the *1.SS-Reitersturm* of the *7.SS-Reiter-Standarte*. Four days later, at the age of eighteen, he was designated as a volunteer cadet for the *SS-Verfugüngstruppe*. Peiper enered the *SS-VT* on 23 January 1934 as an *SS-Mann*. On 7 September that same year he was promoted to the rank of *SS-Sturmmann* and on 10 October to *SS-Rottenführer*. In January 1935 he was assigned to the Jüterborg training center. On 1 March 1935 he was promoted to the rank of *SS-Unterscharführer*. On 24 April of the same year he was chosen to attend the officer's course at the *SS-Junkerschule* at Braunschweig. After having attended the officer course and a further course for platoon leaders at the school at Dachau, Peiper was promoted on 20 April 1936 to the rank of *SS-Unterstumführer*, in the *11.Sturm* of

SS-Usftuf. Peiper in the spring of 1936.

the *III.Sturmbann* of the *Leibstandarte SS Adolf Hitler*. That which would later become the *11.Kp./LSSAH* was called the "moonlight" company because its commander, Carl Marcks, was in the habit of training his men particularly at night. Between 1936 and 1938 Peiper continued his military training and travelled extensively throughout all of Europe. On 30 January 1939 he was promoted to *SS-Obersturmführer* and for the first time left the *Leibstandarte*. He had in fact been selected by the *Reichsführer-SS*, Heinrich Himmler, to serve on his personal staff, as liaison officer of the *SS-VT*. On 29 June 1939, Jochen Peiper married Sigurd Hinrichsen, one of Himmler's secretaries. From their marriage two girls were born, Elke and Silke, and one boy, Hinrich.

Nuremberg 1936: Himmler shaking hands with Peiper before awarding the SS-Ehrendegen, the dagger issued to SS officers.

SS-Ustuf. Peiper, in parade dress uniform, during a ceremony with other members of the 11./LSSAH.

At War

On 3 September 1939, Peiper joined Himmler's staff at the Berlin railway station. There, there were three special trains, for Hitler, Göring and Himmler. During the night, the trains moved on towards Silesia and stopped near the border with Poland. From there, Peiper was able to follow the advance of the units of his *Leibstandarte Adolf Hitler*.

In early March 1940, Peiper returned to active duty in the *LSSAH*, assuming command of the *11.Kompanie* and taking part in the campaign on the Western Front. Peiper's baptism of fire came on 25 March, during an attack against Mount Watten, near Dunkirk.

The *Leibstandarte* began its attack against Mount Watten at 7:00, following a brief artillery shelling by the *IV./SS-Art.Rgt* and by the *16.(s.IG)Kp/LSSAH*. The *10.Kp./LSSAH* led y *SS-Hstuf.* Weidenhaupt attacked on the right and the *11.Kp./LSSAH* under *SS-Ostuf.* Peiper on the left. Despite being lightly wounded in the head by some shell splinters, Peiper distinguished himself in the fighting, successfully leading his men in the assault. For that action and other actions that followed in the area of Vichy, on 31 May Peiper was awarded the Iron Cross Second Class and on 1 June 1940 with the First Class. Also on 1 June he was promoted to the rank of *SS-Hauptsturmführer*.

On 20 June 1940 Peiper was recalled to Himmler's staff, this time as adjutant and *Waffen SS* liaison officer. On 10 July 1940 he accompanied Himmler to the Berghof, where Hitler and his generals would decide what their next moves should be. In October 1940 Karl Wolff, Jochen Peiper and Heinrich Himmler were received by Generalissimo Francisco Franco during an official visit to Spain. On 14 November, Peiper was promoted to Himmler's principal adjutant.

With the beginning of Operation "Barbarossa", in June 1941, desiring to return to combat, Peiper requested to be transferred again to the *Leibstandarte*. And thus, in July 1941, Peiper returned to take command of his *11.Kompanie*, distinguishing himself in the fighting on the Dnieper front, on the Don, and pursuing the Soviet forces along the shores of the Sea of Azov. During this fighting, *SS-Hstuf.* Peiper was slightly wounded in his right knee and suffered the rupture of his eardrums following a loud explosion. After a brief period of rest and convalescence he returned once again to the front line, passing the winter of 1941/42 with *Leibstandarte* units on the Eastern front.

May 1939: Himmler, Hitler and Paul Hausser viewing maneuvers of the Deutschland regiment at Münsterlager. To the right, the aide-de-camp to the Reichsführer-SS, SS-Ostuf. Peiper, can be seen.

France, June 1940: Peiper on the right, along with Sepp Dietrich with the dog, and on the left, Kurt "Panzer" Meyer.

Russia, winter 1941: Peiper scanning the front line.

Reorganization of the Leibstandarte in France

On July 1942, it was decided to withdraw the *Leibstandarte* from the Eastern Front, to reorganize it as a full division, as a *Panzergrenadier* division. The transformation took place between August and December of 1942. On 14 September, Joachim Peiper assumed command of the *III./SS-Inf.Rgt. 2 "LSSAH"*, replacing Günther Anhalt. He installed his headquarters in a small castle near Verneuil-sur-Avre. As a first step, it was necessary to re-form the motorcycle reconnaissance platoons, the *Kraderkundugszug*, which had been disbanded in the Ukraine. The new platoons were equipped with BMW R-75 machines with sidecars.

On 24 November 1942, by Hitler's order, the *Leibstandarte* was officially transformed into a *Panzergrenadier* division and officially named as the *SS-Panzer-Grenadier-Division "LSSAH"*. At the same time, Peiper's *III./2* was transformed into a motorized infantry battalion, equipped with armored vehicles for the infantrymen (*Schützenpanzerwagen* or SPW, of the *SdKfz.251 Ausf. C* type). This transformation led to a radical transformation of the unit, both in its structure as well as in its tactical employment. Its main task was to support the division's tank regiment when it attacked, being the only "mobile" infantry unit. Experience gained in earlier campaigns had shown that, in fact, normal infantry units were not able to keep up with the rapid advance of the panzers, and this prevented rapidly establishing control over the ground and positions that had been captured. The armored "grenadiers", riding in their half-tracks, not only were able to closely follow the armored units, but were also better protected against any enemy attacks during offensive actions. Each company of the new battalion was equipped with eighteen SPW (*Spähpanzerwagen*) vehicles, divided into three platoons, each with four SPW, one of which was armed with a 37mm gun, and a heavy platoon with four SPW.

In late 1942, Peiper was granted a leave and was able to travel to see his family. On 30 January 1943, Peiper was promoted to the rank of *SS-Sturmbannführer*.

Cover of the "Stuttgarter Illustrierte" magazine, January 1941.

26 August 1941: Peiper assisting Sepp Dietrich in presenting the first Iron Crosses to soldiers of the Leibstandarte.

Peiper with Himmler during an official visit to Russia, 1941.

Ukraine, February-March 1943

In January 1943, the *Leibstandarte* was transferred to the Eastern Front, in the Ukraine, in the Kharkov sector, to be employed as part of the *SS-Panzerkorps* during the bitter defensive battles and to face the Soviet counteroffensive. *SS-Stubaf.* Peiper's men were

Peiper and Wisch studying maps prior to an action.

engaged in a difficult relief operation, behind enemy lines, to save the men of the *320.Infanterie-Divis*ion, withdrawing towards Smijew. In the evening of 11 February 1943, the *320.Inf.Div.* was ordered to withdraw towards Sidki, along the railway line, to make contact with *Kampfgruppe Peiper*, consisting of *III. (gep.)*/2, reinforced with seven assault guns, coming from the west. Peiper's men had left Podolchow during the night between 11 and 12 February at 4:30. Around 5:00, the *Kampfgruppe* crossed the enemy lines in the sector defended by the *I./2*. Near the bridge that led to Krasnaya Polyana, several groups of Soviet soldiers were wiped out. The march resumed, but soon after, the resupply column was attacked by the enemy and six trucks were lost. At 6:40 the *Kampfgruppe* reached Smijew, taking up positions along the Donetz River. Let us listen to Peiper's own account: *"A few moments later, General Postel appeared in a large vehicle Along with some other officers. He asked me why we had not yet crossed the river. My explanation that the ice covered surface would not support the weight of our vehicles was at first not accepted, but soon after an officer confirmed it. He reported that "Herr General, the ice is not thick enough, the first assault gun is already immobilized". General Postel was in good*

humor. He told us that he would set up his headquarters on the spot and that we had to provide security for him. He was very disturbed that our lines were so far away. Then he disappeared. After a long pause, the division appeared. Sitting in our SPW, we had passed this lapse of time with

Half-tracks of Kampfgruppe Peiper on the move.

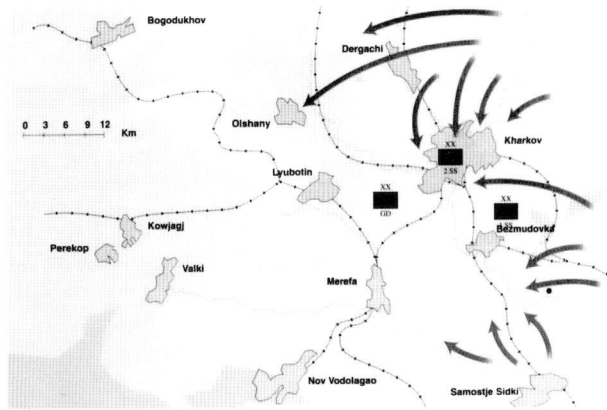

Soviet offensive thrusts north and south of Kharkov.

An SdKfz 251/9 "Stummel" of Kampfgruppe Peiper.

A German infantry unit crossing a frozen river, February 1943.

Peiper on board his SPW.

Kampfgruppe Peiper vehicles moving through a village in flames.

Men of III.(gep.)/2 at a halt during a battle.

unpleasant feelings. We had all had the same impression: the memory of Beresina! Napoleon's retreat…the soldiers who were able to march were in the lead, then followed the lightly wounded and finally those more seriously wounded. A column of misery on carts and trailers of all types…Our doctors and surgeons quickly took care of the most urgent cases. The wounded were the first to be fed and to be given a warm soup. I still remember our surgeon, Doctor Brüstle, who shared his bitterness with me the next morning. He and his assistant had operated throughout the night and not one doctor from the 320.Inf.Div. had helped them… the next day (13 February), the never-ending column resumed its march. The division with all of its wounded along the road and us, on both sides of it, to protect them. When we reached close to the narrows with its long wooden bridge, nothing but the supports remained of the structure.

A battalion of Soviet skiers had occupied the village and had massacred numerous German drivers and doctors. Shells began to fall on the column from all sides. My battalion captured the village, house by house, established a bridgehead and allowed our comrades to come over from the other side, after having repaired the bridge or crossing directly over the frozen surface of the river. After the last of our vehicles had crossed to the opposite bank, my battalion SPW turned around and went back to Smijew to reach our lines…".

Leibstandarte officers on the Ukrainian front, February 1943.

Peiper in the company of Otto Dinse, bottom, and Heinz von Westernhagen.

SS-Stubaf. Peiper on board his command vehicle. (NA)

Around 16:00, the column of ambulances with about 750 wounded reached the German lines. The last elements of the *320.Inf.Div.* crossed the bridge at Krasnaya Polyana the next day at 7:00.

Peiper had developed a special tactic, to attack villages occupied by the enemy at night, attacking them from all sides, with his half-tracks at full speed, shooting at every house or building. This method quickly resulted in the entire village being set afire and created panic among the enemy forces. Peiper's unit thus earned the title *of Lötlampe Bataillon*, or the "blowtorch battalion". The symbol of a blowtorch was painted on the unit's vehicles.

On 12 February, at 3:00, the *III.(gep.)/2* began to pull back towards the area of Merefa, crossing through Kharkov, which was already ablaze. Around noontime Peiper was ordered to return, towards Kharkov, to eliminate Soviet units that had made it as far as Ossnowa, a neighborhood of the city. After having completed the mission, which was not without its problems, Peiper continued the withdrawal towards Merefa. On 15 February, *III.(gep.)/2* took up positions at Komarowka, digging into defensive positions. On 17 February, he was ordered to block an enemy penetration to the south of Udy. After having been in reserve for the entire day of

A column of III.(gep.)/2 half-tracks on the Ukrainian front, February 1943.

Peiper with the Ritterkreuz.

SS-Stubaf. Peiper in conference with SS-Hstuf. Georg Bormann.

the 18th in the Krasnograd area, on the afternoon of 19 February Peiper's *III.(gep.)/2* was ordered to attack towards Jeremejewka, on two axes. During the fighting southeast of Ziglerowka, *III.(gep.)/2* completely wiped out an enemy infantry battalion and captured or destroyed eleven anti-tank guns, three tanks and fifteen mortars.

At dawn on 20 February, *III.(gep.)/2* resumed its attack, taking Jeremejewka at 6:30. Peiper's SPW then pursued the enemy rifle regiment that had defended the town. Soon after the clashes, Peiper made his report: the Soviets had lost three tanks, twelve anti-tank guns, one infantry support gun, two trucks, fifteen mortars and had left seven hundred and fifty dead on the field.

The Knight's Cross

The German offensive to recapture Kharkov began on 6 March: the *SS-Panzerkorps* divisions threw themselves into the attack towards the northeast, with the *Totenkopf* on the left, the *Das Reich* on the right and the *Leibstandarte* in the center. At 8:20, the *II./SS-Pz.Gr.Rgt.2 "LAH"* took the position at Ljachowa, after heavy fighting in the streets and among the houses, and despite the delayed support by the artillery. Peiper's *III.(gep.)/2* took advantage of this success to establish a bridgehead on the Msha River, near Bridok and Federowka at 14:30. Less than an hour later, *SS-Stubaf.* Peiper reported by radio that enemy forces that had been put to flight by the advance of

Peiper on board his command vehicle. (NA)

Peiper speaking with Teddy Wisch.

Men of Kampfgruppe Peiper in action on the outskirts of Khakov, engaged in the final assault against the city.

Half-tracks of III.(gep.)/2 on the move towards Kharkov, March 1943.

Peiper having a happy discussion with SS-Stubaf. Heinz von Westernhagen.

I. and *II./2* had been intercepted and cut to pieces by his battalion. For this action, Peiper was recommended for the Knight's Cross by *SS-Ogruf.* Dietrich, which was officially awarded to him on 9 March 1943. Following is the text of his commendation:

"SS-Sturmbannführer *Peiper, commander of* III. (gep.)SS-Pz.Gr.Rgt.2, *on 6 March 1943, after having stood against the enemy attack along the line Prossjandje-Hf.Ljaschowa-Gawrilowka, was given the mission to carry out an advance against Hf. Peressel. At 11:45, having left from his own lines, he reached the southern edge of Peressel at 13:45 hours. From there, at 14:00, he attacked and seized the enemy position, then, on his own initiative, continued the attack past the original objective. Around 15:30 hours he had infiltrated into the strong enemy field positions that were organized to defend the Federowka-Hf.Bridok sector, establishing a bridgehead. He held this bridgehead despite the fact that it was cut off from all contact with the rear area and was attacked by very large enemy forces. During the fighting, three T-34 tanks were destroyed. With this action,* SS-Sturmbannführer *Peiper set the stage for the subsequent attack, which occurred on 7 March 1943…*".

On 9 March, the SS troops continued to be employed to wipe out enemy units west of Kharkov; at dawn, *III.(gep.)/2* crossed through Ljubotin and made contact with *SS-Pz.Gr.Rgt.1* at Komuna. At 11:00, Peiper's men attacked Bogaty, literally tearing a Soviet battalion to shreds. At 18:15, at the moment he was told that he had been awarded the Knight's Cross, Peiper reported that over the course of the day he had inflicted the following losses to the enemy: twenty-three Katyusha rocket launchers, two 122mm howitzers, four 45mm guns, seven mortars, twenty-five trucks and two hundred fifty killed. Losses for *III.(gep.)/2* were only one killed and two wounded.

In the evening, the units under Fritz Witt and Kurt Meyer reached northeast of Kharkov, advancing towards Zirkuny, while Peiper's men were approaching Dergatschi. Until 12 March, all of the *Leibstandarte* units were engaged in bitter and decisive combat: around 10:30, Jochen Peiper's *III.(gep.)/2* managed to establish contact with *SS-Staf.* Franz Witt's regiment along the main road and then with the grenadiers of *SS-Stubaf.* Max Hansen at Kharkov's Red Square, soon renamed as "*Platz der Leibstandarte*".

The article which appeared in the magazine "Das Schwarze Korps

The *Führer* has conferred the Knight's Cross of the Iron Cross to *SS-Sturmbannführer* Peiper, a battalion commander in the *SS-Panzer-Grenadier-Division "Leibstandarte Adolf Hitler"*.

Das Ritterkreuz für ⚡⚡-Sturmbannführer Peiper

Der Führer verlieh das Ritterkreuz des Eisernen Kreuzes an ⚡⚡-Sturmbannführer Peiper, Bataillonskommandeur in der ⚡⚡-Panzergrenadier-Division „Leibstandarte-⚡⚡ Adolf Hitler".

Half-tracks of III.(gep.)/2 in Kharkov. Peiper;'s vehicle is in the foreground.

Peiper and Fritz Witt in Kharkov.

Another photo of Peiper and Witt in Kharkov.

SS-P.K. Around mid-February, *SS-Sturmbannführer* Peiper, commanding a motorized battalion, was given the mission of making contact with General Postel's *Kampfgruppe*, which according to a *Werhmacht* report, after several days under enemy fire, had had many of its men wounded. The mission of Peiper's battalion, reinforced by several assault guns, was mainly to save a truck convoy loaded with our wounded, passing through the enemy lines.

It has remained unknown if the Bolsheviks were surprised by the unexpected advance by the battalion or if they believed the small *Kampfgruppe* to be the leading element of a larger formation. In any case, the operation went ahead smoothly. The crossing and the breakthrough of the enemy lines went off without any real contact with enemy troops. After the wounded men were some thirty kilometers behind enemy lines, they received the treatment they were in need of. During the nighttime calm, the battalion, which had formed a defensive perimeter, had seen to the protection of the convoy, without too much of a rough ride, of the wounded of *Kampfgruppe Postel*. In the meantime a large force of the enemy had occupied a small village and its adjacent road and had taken possession of the small bridge that connected to the area. *SS-Sturmbannführer* Peiper attacked the village, meeting and quickly destroying a Bolshevik ski unit that had faced off against the battalion. Subsequently, he seized the bridge, enabling the ambulance convoy to cross it.

Kharkov, March 1943: From the left, SS-Stubaf. Weidenhaupt, SS-Stubaf. Peiper and SS-Staf. Witt, in his car.

A team of Leibstandarte machine gunners in the streets of Kharkov, with one of the new MG-42.

A drop of alcohol, to celebrate victory and to warm up a bit.

Continuing onward, they ran into two frozen areas where, however, the thin ice preventing the battalion's heavy vehicles from crossing

Considering this problem, the battalion changed its course, bypassing the enemy and making an exhausting march over difficult terrain, finally reaching the German lines. Later, *SS-Sturmbannfüher* Peiper took an active part in preparations for and development of the attack against Kharkov, managing by his own initiative to establish two bridgeheads which served to infiltrate the assault forces. The measures adopted for these undertakings proved to be excellent, as in the following days the enemy bloodied himself against our defensive line. The surprise of the infiltration had been decisive and the enemy, completely unprepared, had allowed a large booty of weapons and supplies fall into the hands of the battalion. As witness to this extremely dramatic fighting, it is appropriate to say that wherever his battalion found itself, water was thrown on the fire. *SS-Sturmbannfüher* Peiper was the man for the occasion, as he was present in all phases of the fighting. The officers of the units called upon him for support, which inevitably resulted in success.

This was the reason they were happy to see him show up in their sectors. The feeling that had been created now, in every officer and man of *Kampfgruppe Peiper*, was that by strictly following the decisions and orders he gave, everything would be fine. This thought was enough to increase their fearlessness and courage that the men showed in the field in the face of difficulties. This intellectual peace of mind that instilled itself in every one of them gave them the strength to face any adversity. The commander himself also had a bit of luck. His absolute faith in his men was however based on something more concrete than his own feelings, which spring from a conscientious and responsible officer; the concern for the loss of each single man, can go even beyond what is necessary. Orders, however, often do not come as a result of subtle meditation, but from the brain and the heart of the man himself.

The good sense and the hands of these soldiers are always bound together, they do not always think in a knowing and constructive manner and at times only for their own personal satisfaction, but they separate duty from their daily life, remaining always and only soldiers of the Party. This young, but experienced thirty-eight year old commander, who for some time had also been the personal aide-de-camp of the *Reichsführer-SS*, was born in Berlin Wilmersdorf on 30 January 1915, participated in the Polish campaign and that on the

SS-Stubaf. Peiper with the Ritterkreuz.

Western Front and was awarded the Iron Cross Second Class in May 1940 and the First Class in July 1940 (*SS-Kriegsberichter* Dr. Arthur Wenn).

The recapture of Bjelgorod

Following the recapture of Kharkov, the units of the *Leibstandarte* were engaged in a new attack towards Bjelgorod. In the lead was Peiper's *III.(gep.)/2* and the tanks of the *7.Kp./SS-Pz.Rgt. "LAH"* under *SS-Ostuf.* Rudolf von Ribbentrop. The attack began on 17 March; the rough terrain conditions slowed down the advance of the SS tanks and half-tracks. During the next night, *Kampgruppe Peiper* was stalled along the road to Kassatschjlopan by a Soviet anti-tank screen, south of Nechotejewka. At dawn on 18 March, *SS-Stubaf.* Peiper attacked the enemy positions between Krestowo and Naumowka, running into strong enemy resistance there. Support by Stukas was needed to be able to breach the enemy lines. At ten in the morning, Peiper's men reached Krasnoye and a hour later he was able to report via

Peiper and Otto Dinse, conferring with another officer, during the attack on Bjelgorod.

SdKfz 251 of Peiper's III.(gep.)/2.

A half-track of III.(gep.)/2 on the march towards Bjelgorod.

A Panzer of the Leibstandarte at Bjelgorod.

SS-Sturmbannführer Jochen Peiper.

radio that "*...I am only eight kilometers southwest of Bjelgorod. The Soviet units are fleeing!*". The attack continued and at 11:15 Peiper again reported by radio that "*...Bjelgorod has been taken. Eight tanks have been destroyed*". Peiper's attack caught the Soviets completely by surprise and when *III.(gep.)/2*, reinforced by two Tiger tanks, broke through the forward defensive line most of the enemy soldiers were still resting. It was not until around noon that the enemy attempted a desperate counterattack, employing an armored formation northwest of Bjelgorod. The *11.Kp./2*, led by *SS-Hstuf.* Paul Guhl, positioned along the course of the Donetz, rebuffed the Soviet tank attack, destroying at least six enemy tanks in the ferocious defensive battle. In the afternoon contact was finally made with troops of the *Grossdeutschland* at Dolbino and Novaya Derewenja. *Kampfgfruppe Peiper* was then ordered to secure the access points north and west of Bjelgorod in order to rebuff any eventual enemy counterattacks. That same evening, Peiper rendered a report on the losses inflicted upon the enemy: 14 tanks, 16 guns, 14 anti-tank rifles, 52 machine guns and 38 trucks. The Germans had suffered only one killed and six wounded.

The German Cross in Gold

On 6 May 1943, *SS-Stubaf.* Peiper was awarded the German Cross in Gold. Let us see the citation written by *SS-Ogruf.* Sepp Dietrich: "*... The III Battalion of the 2nd Panzergrenadier regiment of the* "Leibstandarte Adolf Hitler"*, commanded by* SS-Sturmbannführer *Peiper, located on the right wing of the division, was one of the first to join in the fighting that was going on near the Kharkov railway station. The mission, of primary importance, was to establish a support position at Andrejewka and at the same time to create a position to favor the breakthrough by units of the 320.Infanterie-Division. Despite the fact that on 7 February 1943 his unit had been surrounded by large Soviet forces (two rifle regiments and a tank brigade),* SS-Stubaf. *Peiper completed his mission. After two days of combat, during which his position was reinforced despite being surrounded, Peiper broke the ring of the enemy main combat line* (HauptKampf Linie) *surrounding him and was able to bring has battalion back. In completing his mission, he inflicted heavy losses to the enemy, among which were two T-34 tanks. In this situation,* SS-Stubaf. *Peiper distinguished himself by displaying his authority and personal courage in the field.*

Following the withdrawal of the units along the general line Rogan-Lisogubowka-Mirgorod, Peiper was assigned the mission to attack and seize the position at Smijew with his battalion and to establish a secure link with the 320. Infanterie-Division. Peiper carried out the order and along the corridor that was created was able to bring back to his own lines 750 wounded men of the 320.Inf.Div. In this period, with his battalion, he scattered a battalion of enemy skiers that was attempting to infiltrate. When the SS-Div. "Das Reich" had halted to set up a new defensive line, Peiper was tasked with ensuring that the men of that division could work uninterruptedly. On this occasion also, while fighting as a rearguard, Peiper displayed his style of command.

From Starowerowka, the battalion was ordered to take Ziglerowka. The mission was completed after having run into stiff enemy resistance and having destroyed and scattered an enemy battalion, in addition to four 76.2mm guns, an infantry support gun, ten mortars and machine guns, and numerous other weapons. The material was either destroyed or captured.

Soon after, Peiper continued the advance, going past Kasatchi Majdan; an enemy battalion that was deployed along the breakthrough line clashed with Peiper's troops and was soon overrun. On this occasion as well, enemy losses were high and they did not prevent the seizure of Kasatchi Majdan. From there, Peiper and his battalion were made available for a fresh advance against Jeremejewka. At dawn, it attacked the position at Jeremejewka that was defended by strong hostile forces and occupied it. Taking advantage of the enemy's confusion, the battalion continued its advance to Leninskiy, breaking the back of the last Russian resistance. The field to the east was now free and the enemy fled in disorder. The battalion pursued the enemy inflicting heavy losses upon him. The battalion had destroyed: 2 T-34 tanks and one light tank, six 7.62 cm guns, 300 horses were captured and three columns formed by sleds were destroyed. Enemy dead amounted to some 800-900 men.

The examples given show that SS-Sturmbannfuhrer *Peiper, by the personal valor shown while commanding his battalion in the face of the enemy, is worthy of receiving the German Cross in Gold.*".

Operation "Zitadelle"

Preparations for Operation *Zitadelle*, the elimination of the Kursk salient, began as early as 28 June 1943. The *units of SS-Pz.Gren.Div. "LSSAH"* reached their assembly areas on the night of 2 July. At that time, the division had eleven Tiger tanks, seventy-two PzKpfw IV, sixteen PzKpfw II and thirty-one assault guns. Enemy forward outposts were eliminated during the night of 4 July, while men of the *LSSAH* moved to their departure positions. Peiper's battalion, *III.(gep.)/2*, was assigned to the *Leibstandarte* armored group. At 3:10 on 5 July 1943, the SS units moved from the area west of Bjelgorod towards the north, towards

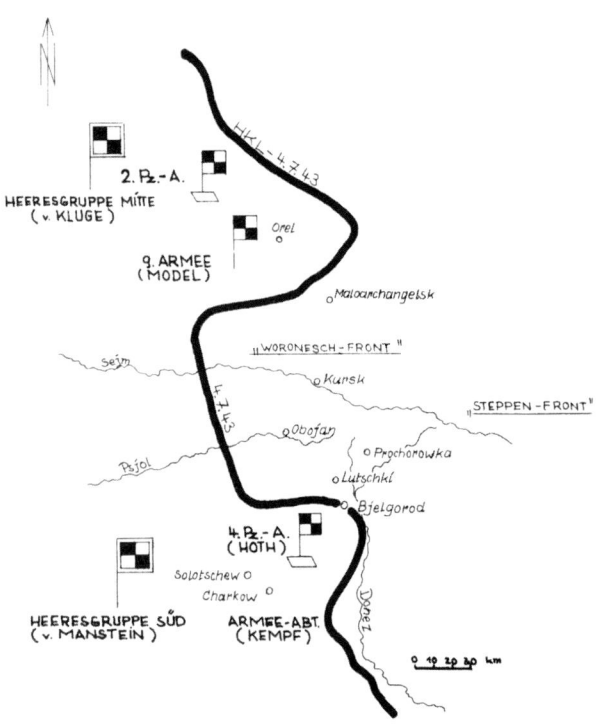

Situation of the opposing forces on 4 July 1943.

SS-Stubaf. Peiper during the fighting at Kursk.

A column of LSSAH half-tracks on the move.

24

Two photos of a Leibstandarte SdKfz.251/10 in the Kursk area, armed with a 37mm anti-tank gun. (NA)

SS-Ustuf. Werner Wolff and SS-Stubaf. Peiper at Kursk.

SS grenadiers passing by a destroyed T-34.

A PzKpfw III engaged in the Prokhorovka area.

Bykovka. Thanks to air support, the SS soldiers broke through the Soviet forward defensive line, engaging in furious hand-to-hand combat with the enemy. On the afternoon of 6 July, after having passed through Lutshi Teterevino, Peiper's battalion attacked. Deployed across a wide attack front, the half-tracks travelled at full speed towards an anti-tank ditch protected by minefields and defended by anti-tank guns and tanks. After a bitter battle, Peiper's men succeeded in getting past the Soviet defenses and capture Teterevino. The Soviets counterattacked soon after with armored units, but Peiper's battalion held out and destroyed at least five enemy tanks. During the night of 7 July, a Tiger tank that had arrived as a reinforcement destroyed three more Soviet tanks. The next morning, the SS armored group attacked along the Teterevino-Prokhorovka road. A furious battle erupted between tanks beginning at 7:00 and lasted until the afternoon. Peiper and his motorized battalion had taken up positions in front of elements of *II./SS-Pz.Rgt. "LSSAH"*. Shortly after, Peiper's men moved forward and were surrounded by enemy forces. The *7.Panzerkompanie* was sent to the rescue, but was unable to make contact with Peiper's men because of the strong enemy superiority. *SS-Stubaf.* Peiper then decided to free his battalion by himself, managing to open up an escape route, fighting strongly against the enemy.

Kursk, July 1943: On the left, Peiper on board his command vehicle during the fighting, and on the right, while he presents the Iron Cross Second Class to one of his grenadiers in the presence of SS-Ustuf. Werner Wolff. (NA)

On 9 July 1943, continuing their advance, Peiper's motorized battalion found itself again facing a Soviet position strongly defended by anti-tank guns and tanks. The SS half-tracks, lightly protected, were easy targets for the enemy anti-tank guns. Acting on his own initiative and against the orders from his battalion commander, *SS-Stubaf.* Martin Gross, the *6.Panzerkompanie*, led by *SS-Ostuf.* Rudolf von Ribbentrop, joined in the fighting and saved Peiper's men from that difficult situation. Von Ribbentrop's tanks knocked out six enemy tanks, thus removing the threat to the flank of the SS battalion.

On 11 July, the terrible battle began in the area of Prokhorovka; around 10:15 Peiper and his battalion moved forward and got as far as the southern part of Hill 252.5, Shortly after, a *Luftwaffe* plane destroyed a half-track belonging to the battalion, despite the presence of a liaison officer in Peiper's command vehicle. The SPW battalion got past Hill 252.5, and during the night preparations were made

Another photo of Peiper during the fighting at Kursk, July 1943.

A German soldier with a Mauser rifle with a grenade launcher attached. (NA)

for the attack towards Prokhorovka. On 12 July, the biggest tank battle in history began. The Soviets had fielded two new tank corps against the three German divisions of the *SS-Panzerkorps*. Throughout the day, the *Leibstandarte* armored group was attacked by at least fifty enemy tanks along the line Prokhorovka-Petrovka. Peiper's SPW battalion found itself at the center of the enemy attack.

Peiper's aide, *SS-Ustuf.* Werner Wolf, assumed command of a company that had lost its leader and fought desperately against the unexpected and massive armored penetration. More than thirty enemy tanks were destroyed during the course of the fighting at close range, and during the afternoon the earlier line of resistance was re-established. *SS-Stubaf.* Peiper was also involved in the fighting at close range against the Soviet tanks, using a various assortment of weapons including hand grenades, anti-tank mines and Molotov cocktails. Peiper's actions were related in an article that appeared in a newspaper of the era:"*The dust and smoke had become so thick that they brought tears to the eyes.*

This yellow cloud obscured the vision and from it emerged the enormous shapes of Soviet tanks drawing ever closer, grey shadows that headed towards us. A loud bang was suddenly heard on the right; the commander was bent on his knees, a rifle pressed against his shoulder. The barrel, onto which a grenade launcher had been mounted, followed the rapid movement of a T-34. With its engine rumbling and its tracks screeching, the tank was headed towards him, crossing ditches that were three meters deep. At that instant, the commander's rifle grenade was let loose and hit the tank between the turret and the hull. The tank continued on for another twenty or thirty meters, then stopped, shuddering. Smiling happily, the Sturmbannführer *yelled to his men:* "Today we'll earn the close-quarter combat badge, my soldiers.[1]"

For this action, Peiper was awarded the tank-killer's badge, the *Panzervernichtungsabzeichen*.[2]

---

[1] Some texts also recount another version: during encounters in the Kursk area, on 12 July 1943, Soviet tank units broke through the *Leibstandarte's* lines. *SS-Stubaf.* Jochen Peiper found himself alone, facing a T-34. Waiting for a favorable moment, he jumped on the turret, opened the hatch, and threw in a hand grenade, killing the entire enemy crew.

[2] The complete deignation *is Sonderabzeichen für das Niederkämpfen von Panzerkampfwagen durch Einselkämpfer*, or, Special Badge for the Destruction of a Tank with Individual Weapons. For each enemy tank or vehicle destroyed, a Silver Badge was awarded. During the course of the war, it became common to be awarded several badges, so on 18 December 1943, a version in gold was instituted.

Transfer to Italy

A few days before the Italian capitulation, Peiper paraded his unit, disarmed, through the streets of Reggio Emilia. In the two photos, Peiper is between SS-Hstuf. Paul Guhl and SS-Ustuf. Werner Wolff with the Knight's Cross. (DWS)

Reggio Emilia, August 1943: SS-Stubaf. Peiper reviewing his troops. Note on the right sleeve of the uniform the tank killer's badge and on the right pocket the German Cross in Gold.

On 18 July 1943, Peiper and his battalion marched towards Bjelgorod and were loaded aboard a railway convoy. On 26 July, they reached Stalino, where the tanks were offloaded to be assigned to the *Totenkopf*. On 29 July, orders arrived for a transfer to Italy, where the political situation was deteriorating and called for the presence of faithful and reliable military forces, ready to intervene. On 31 July 1943, the *Leibstandarte* division commander, *SS-Ogruf.* Sepp Dietrich, met with field Marshal Erwin Rommel at the headquarters of Army Group B in northern Italy.

An SdKfz.250 of III.(gep.)/2 in Italy.

In anticipation of the imminent Italian defection, the *Leibstandarte* was ordered to prepare to carry out the following missions: ensure control of the roads between the Brenner Pass and Verona and disarm Italian troops in the Po Plain area if necessary. Peiper and his battalion reached Innsbruck on 1 August 1943 and from there, they moved with their vehicles as far as Trento on 8 August 1943. Around mid-August, most of the men of the *Leibstandarte* took up positions in the Po Plain. On 3 September 1943, the chief of staff of the *II.SS-Pz.Korps*, SS-*Oberführer* Werner Ostendorff, issued dispositions for the disarming and internment of Italian troops. These measures were to be taken after receiving the code word "*Nordwind*". The *Leibstandarte* was tasked with keeping ready a strong combat group to ensure security of the Verona-Brenner road. On 8 September 1943, upon notice of the signing of the armistice between Italy and the Allies, the disarmament of Italian garrisons in all of northern Italy began immediately.

On 10 September, Peiper's SPW battalion was sent to disarm the garrisons at Alessandria and Asti in Piedmont. Soon thereafter, *III.(gep.)/2* moved towards Alba and Bra, where the Italian garrisons were disarmed without incident on 11 September. On 13 September, Peiper conducted reconnaissance in the area of Fossano and Mondovì. On 14 September, with their armored vehicles, the SS troops reached Cuneo. The Italian troops in that city surrendered only after difficult negotiations: at the time, 82 officers and 254 NCOs and Italian soldiers were captured. Most of the Italian troops had withdrawn to the area southwest of Cuneo: most of the soldiers did not know what to do and many desired only to return to their homes and their families as soon as possible. On 16 September, Peiper and his battalion clashed with elements of these fleeing troops, continuing to take prisoners and carrying out the disarmament operations.

Boves area, 19 September 1943. Peiper and some of his officers checking the situation next to a Grille self-propelled gun. From the left are SS-Ustuf. Erhard Gührs, SS-Ostuf. Otto Dinse, SS-Ostuf. Rudolf Möhrlin and SS-Stubaf. Peiper with the binoculars.

Self-propelled guns and a Grille of 14.(s.gep.)/SS-Pz.Gren.Rgt.2.

Another photo of Peiper during an action in the Boves area.

The incident at Boves

On 19 September 1943, the Italian police station at Boves reported that two NCOs of the *14.Kp./2* had been captured by soldiers of the Italian 4th Army. *SS-Ostuf.* Otto Dinse[3], the battalion adjutant, was sent to Boves with a truck and an SPW to try to free the men of his company. When he arrived there, he found no one, because the prisoners had been taken to the nearby mountains, south of the city. *SS-Ostuf.* Dinse then tried to flush out the Italian "rebels", asking for help from Peiper. During the first exchanges of fire with the Italian soldiers who had hidden in the mountains, *SS-Sturmmann* Willi Steinmetz was killed. Following is Peiper's own account of the happenings[4]:

"...*I immediately alerted the forces at my disposal[5] and, at the head of my SPW that were moving ahead in combat formation, I headed for Boves. There, we were met by heavy rifle and machine gun fire, coming from houses and the surrounding mountains. The grenades thrown from the mountains were particularly dangerous for our SPW, whose tops were uncovered. My unit suffered losses: in my own SPW, a machine gun burst fired from above killed a radio operator and wounded another soldier, in addition to destroying my radio set. Not being able to see any of the enemy, who were hidden among the houses and the surrounding mountains, I ordered my unit to fall back as far as the entrance to the village, because the SPW were not suited to fighting in the streets. In order to prepare a rapid crossing through the city towards my surrounded comrades, I ordered my "Grillen"[6] to open fire against the houses facing us. Many houses caught fire as a result of the shelling. Under cover of clouds of smoke that had formed, the enemy, in uniform and in civilian clothes, withdrew from that area, accessible only by a narrow defile between the mountains and which was not visible from our positions. The surrounded troops could thus withdraw and join up with us. In the meantime, because the fire was spreading rapidly to the rest of the village, we continued our attack past the narrow defile that limited our visibility. Despite the use of heavy weapons, enemy resistance vanished; behind the defile we came upon six trucks that had been abandoned in firing positons and saw soldiers and civilians firing from the mountains. Upon our return to Cuneo, the Italian prefect, General Salvi, expressed to me his profound excuses for the incident at Boves and disassociated himself, in the name of his government, from the events, naming the Communist parties as the responsible parties. The next day I sent one of my companies to Peveragno, another location where groups of armed enemy rebels had been reported.*

---

[3] Otto Dinse, born on 24 October 1912 in Hamburg, SS Number 10 389. He had served previously in *17./LSSAH*.
[4] Rudolf Lehmann, *Die Leibstandarte, Vol.III*, pages 317-319.
[5] Around eighty men and several armored vehicles.

[6] The name given to 150mm s.IG33 infantry guns mounted on the chassis of Panzer 38(t) tanks, also known as "*Bison*"

Houses in Boves destroyed by fire.

The town of Boves in flames, after the action by German troops.

To my satisfaction, the mayor of that locality, who had great influence over his fellow citizens who were still armed, categorically distanced himself from the actions of Allied agents and we thus reached an agreement to avoid further incidents. I am convinced that by our intervention at Boves to free our surrounded comrades we caused units of the Italian 4th Army to disband and avoided attacks against Cuneo and Turin. It is true that the action caused victims among the civilian population of Boves, but avoided the useless shedding of blood…"

After the war, around twenty-five years later, Peiper, Dinse and Gührs were accused by the Italian authorities of the deaths of twenty-four civilians at Boves at the court in Stuttgart. At that time the verdict established that there was not sufficient evidence to find the accused guilty. Because of conflicting testimony, many doubts were raised as to just how events had transpired. Otto Dinse testified that he had not been surrounded, but only that he had ended up under enemy fire, after which he received orders over the radio to withdraw and to wait at the southern edge of the village. The inquest, conducted by Jens Westmeier[7], revealed that only one SS soldier, Willi Steinmetz, had been killed that day. Thus, had Peiper claimed that his radio operator had been killed only in order to justify the shelling of Boves with fire from the *Grillen*? But, looking at the photos of the houses, their walls appear intact, without any damage from shells, as though the fires had been set from inside. *SS-Ustuf.* Heinz Tomhardt, a platoon leader in *13.Kp./2*, described the events in complete contradiction to Peiper's version[8]: *"This action had begun with the capture of two SS soldiers by the partisans. As far as I was concerned, it was an anti-partisan operation…I remember that were deployed along a narrow path that led to the mountains. We passed through a village, which must have been Boves, but no one shot at us. Later, fire was opened against the leading elements…On the road as we returned, I again crossed through Boves with my armored vehicle. There, I saw German soldiers who were taking things from the shops. I never approved of that type of behavior. In my opinion, there were no fires in Boves. I saw nothing of the kind. We crossed through Boves without stopping for long. I saw no civilians. In my opinion, the village was deserted…I was alone, and as I have already said, I saw no fires and no dead civilians. The encounters took place on the surrounding mountains…"*.

In early October, Peiper's battalion moved to Alessandria, where the new recruits could continue their training. On 20 October 1943, Peiper was awarded the pin or badge for close-quarter combat in Silver. On 25 October, *Leibstandarte* units began to be loaded aboard rail convoys for their transfer to the Eastern front.

---

[7] Jens Westmeier, *Joachim Peiper, A Biography of Himmler's SS Commander*, pages 139-146.

[8] Ibid, page 141.

Ukrainian Front 1943-44

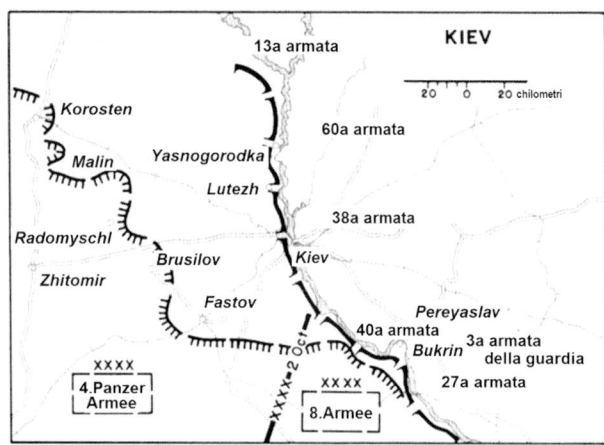

Situation on the Ukrainian front between October and November 1943.

Pieper discussing the situation in the field with his officers.

November 1943: A column of Tiger tanks of the Leibstandarte, passing through a Ukrainian village, bogged down by the mud.

In early November 1943, the leading elements of *Leibstandarte* began to arrive by train in the Zhitomir area. The men were quickly sent to the front line without waiting for the entire division to be assembled. *SS-Stubaf.* Peiper, after having assembled his battalion, was soon engaged in a series of counterattacks in cooperation with other elements of the division. On 17 November, the battalion successfully carried out an attack against Lutchin, with the support of *Leibstandarte* Tiger tanks, eliminating a dangerous threat on the division's flank. On 18 November 1943, along with tanks of the *II.SS-Pz.Rgt.1*, an attack was made against the positions at Morozovka, during which numerous enemy forces were wiped out. On 20 November 1943, the commander *of SS-Pz.Rgt.1, SS-Ostubaf.* Georg Schönberger, was killed after having been hit by a shell fragment during a Soviet artillery bombardment against the command post at Solowjewka. In his place, the division commander, *SS-Oberführer* Teddy Wisch, designated Peiper, even though he had no previous experience with tank units.

In command of SS-Panzer Regiment 1 "LSSAH"

In the official document dated 28 November 1943 proposing promotion, Wisch wrote: "…*After the heroic death of SS-Ostubaf. Schönenberg, SS-Stubaf. Peiper was placed in command of SS-Panzer Regiment 1. He is a simple personality, happy and energetic. He has demonstrated his tactical skills as a battalion commander, demonstrating his ability to take advantage of every opportunity for the division in conducting rapid and mobile advances. This special ability in being able to recognize and exploit favorable situations, along with his determination during counterattacks and with his experience in achieving deep breakthroughs in the enemy's main line of resistance and into his rear areas, render him particularly suited to assume command of a tank regiment, especially because of his extreme personal courage. He is an officer capable of inspiring his men. He has a good attitude towards command and his determination to face battle is a personal characteristic of his*". His nomination was supported by Dietrich as

Jochen Peiper, November 1943.

PzKpfw IV of 5.Kp./SS-Pz.Rgt.1, during an attack against Soviet positions.

well as by Himmler himself. Many members of the *Panzer Regiment* were not at all convinced that Peiper had been the proper choice. There were other officers in the regiment who were held to be more capable, such as *SS-Stubaf.* Martin Gross, commander of *II./SS-Pz.Rgt.1* and decorated with the Knight's Cross, and *SS-Hstuf.* Herbert Kuhlmann, commander of 1./SS-Pz.Rgt.1. In addition, his reputation was not the best. There was talk about villages that had been burnt down on the Eastern Front and about civilians who had been massacred both in Russia as well as in Italy, and much more as well.

The battle raged and there was not much time to think about these rumors. *SS-Stubaf.* Peiper chose a PzKpfw. IV as his command vehicle; the crew usually consisted of *SS-Ostuf.* Helmut Jahn, chief of communications, *SS-Uscha.* Otto Becker, the driver, and two other radio operators, *SS-Uscha.* Fritz Kosmehl and *SS-Sturmmann* Horst Schumann. To show his courage to his tankers, Peiper often conducted operations by climbing aboard other tanks and leaving his command tank so that he could always be in the thick of the fight.

On 23 November, the *LSSAH Panzer-Regiment* moved from the Yastrebenka area, to the northeast, towards Fasowaja. The tanks moved more slowly than his SPW, and Peiper showed himself to be insufferable. He thus gave all of his tank commanders this order: "*Quickly, quickly, move forward!*" Without having sent

November 1943, armored elements of the *Leibstandarte Panzergruppe* moving to attack on the snowy steppe.

33

A column of PzKpfw V Panther tanks of 1./SS-Pz.Rgt.1 on the march on the Ukrainian front, autumn 1943.

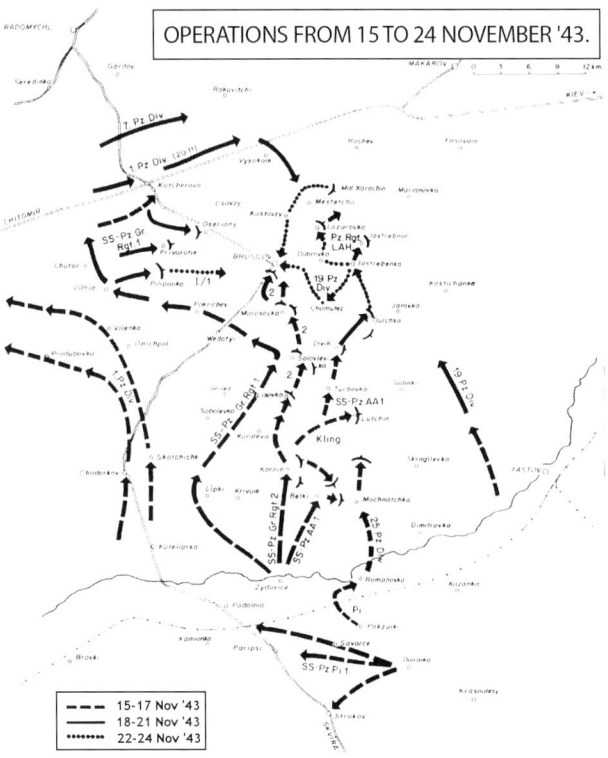

Operations from 15 to 24 November '43.

any reconnaissance patrols ahead, as soon as the tanks approached villages occupied by the enemy, they ended up under fire from Soviet 76.2cm anti-tank guns; six panzers were quickly destroyed. The other tanks continued to move forward and thanks to support by the grenadiers they were able to finally overcome the Soviet resistance. After having taken the villages of Dubrowka and Lasarowka, Peiper sent his tanks against Mestetscho for refueling. The mud and the autumn rains continued to hamper the advance of the SS units.

On 24 November the *Leibstandarte* armored group crossed the Sdwisch River, to launch its attack against Starizkaja. For the operation, the companies of *SS-Pz. Gr.Rgt.2* were attached. The armored group attacked at 12:30, immediately running up against a *Pak-front*, near the western outskirts of Starizkaja. At the same time, a Soviet tank formation attacked on the flank; the SS tanks quickly moved forward, but once again ended up under fire from the Soviet anti-tank guns, incurring heavy losses. During the furious fighting that developed, the Soviets however had the worst of it; Peiper's tanks managed to break through the village, where *SS-Oscha.* Hans Dauser, *Zugführer* of *2.Kp./SS-Pz.Rgt.1*, distinguished himself, who with his tank was able to knock out about thirty Soviet tanks. The attack progressed with much difficulty, and at 15:40, Peiper's armored group was again stalled in front of Hill 185.4, strongly defended by numerous anti-tank guns. In order to dislodge the Soviets from their positions and to enable Peiper's armored group to continue its offensive action, *SS-Pz.Gr.Rgt.2* was brought into action. Thanks to fire support by the divisional artillery regiment's batteries and by the rocket launcher batteries of *Werfer-Regiment 57*, Hill 185.4 was captured by the SS troops.

On 28 November, after having again assembled his units, *Kampfgruppe Peiper*, reinforced by *III.(gep.)/2*, was engaged in the area south of Radomyschi, to head off an attack by the Soviets on the flanks. Thanks to intervention the *Leibstandarte* Tiger tank company, the threat was driven off.

At 5:30 on 29 November, SS troops were engaged in a new offensive action, along the edge of the woods southwest of the *kolkhoz* at Tolstoje, where they caught by surprise an enemy force that was preparing to attack.

SS-Ustuf. Hans Dauser (BDC)

A column of Panthers with grenadiers on board, autumn 1943.

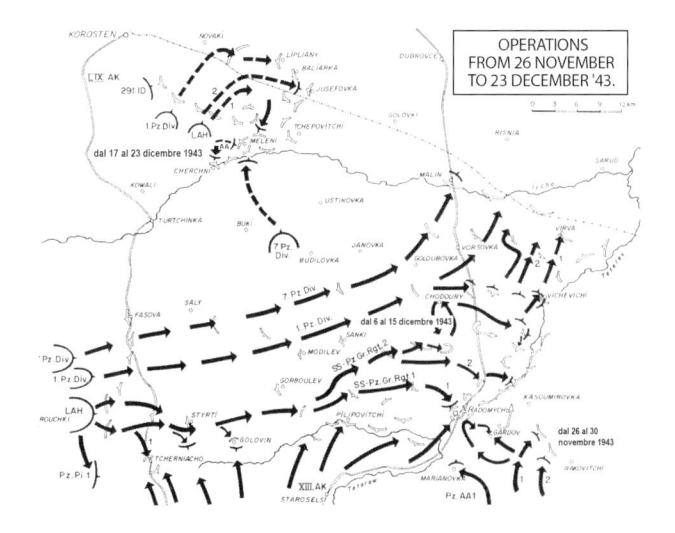

OPERATIONS FROM 26 NOVEMBER TO 23 DECEMBER '43.

Soon after, the half-tracks of *III.(gep.)/2* had to pull back to support *1./SS-Pz.Rgt.1* in its attack against the village of Tolstoje. The SS troops came under Soviet artillery and mortar fire, suffering heavy losses. Only after some forward elements had managed to break into the village was the enemy resistance cut short. Around 9:00, *Kampfgruppe Peiper* attacked and occupied the village of Garboroff.

The offensive continues

After several days of rest, spent mainly in reorganizing the units, on 6 December the *Leibstandarte* resumed its offensive action: the first to move were the grenadiers of

Leibstandarte half-tracks and tanks during a halt, November 1943.

35

Soldiers of *III.(gep.)/2* preparing to attack, December 1943.

Leibstandarte armored cars and half-tracks in a village.

December 1943. *Leibstandarte* tanks and grenadiers.

III.(gep.)/2, who at 4:00 attacked and seized the village of Pekarschtschina. At 6:30, the reconnaissance group attacked the village of Andrejew, then regrouping to the east of that village, to move on towards Styrty. A quarter of an hour later, *I./SS-Pz.Rgt.1* and then *III.(gep.)/2* joined up with the reconnaissance group. At 9:40 the advance elements of *SS-Pz.Gr.Rgt.2* also reached Andrejew, catching the enemy forces by surprise. At 10:30 the position at Styrty was captured by *Kampfgruppe Peiper*. Let us read how the action developed, reading part of the text of the citation for Peiper's Oak Leaves: "...*Based on reconnaissance carried out during the previous night*, SS-Stubaf. Peiper *launched an attack at dawn, and after having wiped out a* Pak*-front, was able to occupy Andrejew around 6:00 and close the road to Korosten-Tschernjachow. To the east of Andrejew, the* Kampfgruppe *destroyed numerous batteries, and at 10:00, after having destroyed numerous anti-tank guns and enemy strongpoints, he reached the hills situated on both sides of Stryrty, the day's objective. With a dashing advance, the* Kampfgruppe *pushed to the east, destroying numerous batteries and anti-tank guns and during its advance, overran the command post of the 121st Rifle Division at Kisselwka, of the 322nd Rifle Division at Selyzchy, of the 148th Rifle Division at Kamenny Brid and of the 336th Rifle Division at Kaitanowka, where it was necessary to stop to resupply. During the course of this day, the* Kampfgruppe *destroyed or captured artillery pieces, 76 7.62cm anti-tank guns, 38 anti-tank rifles, 49 machine guns, 40 vehicles and 71 horse-drawn carts; 1,450 enemy soldiers*

An SS column waiting to be resupplied, December 1943.

SS grenadiers aboard a SdKfz.251/1 armed with an MG34.

Ukraine, December 1943: a formation of PzKpfw IV in the attack.

Panzers and German grenadiers entering a Ukrainian village.

were killed. During this advance, considering the extreme difficulties of employment, the Kampfgruppe *penetrated about thirty kilometers into the enemy's rear area, shaking the entire front. This enabled the* XIII.Armee-Korps *to move forward…".*

In the afternoon, *Kampfgruppe Peiper* reached the railway line east of Tortschin, where it was decided to pause while awaiting resupply. However, shortly after, via radio the division staff ordered that Peiper was to move immediately to Tschaikowa. At the same time, aerial reconnaissance had spotted long Soviet columns that were advancing westward, coming from Tschernjachow. The *Leibstandarte* quickly attacked their flanks, driving away the threat. At 15:05, the engineer battalion was ordered to go to block the road to Tschernjachow to the west, along with the grenadiers of the *I./1*. At 15:20, *SS-Pz.Gr.Rgt.1* resumed its march towards Tschernjachow, while *Kampfgruppe Peiper* was engaged in the sciezure of the position at Kaitanowka. In the late afternoon, Peiper's men were busy eliminating the last nests of resistance in the village of Tortschin. Beginning on 7 December, the Soviets began to react, bringing fresh forces into the sector. That same day, the *Leibstandarte*, after having regrouped its units, sought to continue its offensive operations. At 10:15, the *II./2* led by Rudolf Sandig attacked towards Tschaikowa, but was soon stalled by massive barrier fire unleashed by the enemy from the hills north of Tortschin. Around noon, *SS-Pz.Rgt.1* was engaged south of Tschaikowa to try to support the advance of the *II./2*. But once again, Peiper's tanks were stopped cold by a solid *Pak-front*. At that point, *SS-Obf.* Wisch, at 14:00, ordered *SS-Pz.Rgt.1* to surround the village of Tschaikowa and sent the *Panzerkampfgruppe* to Ljachowa. At 19:00, the *II./2* was finally able to break into the village of Tschaikowa, and after two hours of fighting in the streets and house to house, managed to occupy it. The *Panzerkampfgruppe* instead moved north, capturing the positions at Chodory and Sabolot, during the course of the night and in the morning; during the fighting that ensued, one T-34, eight artillery pieces, sixty-one 7.62cm anti-tank guns, one 4.7cm anti-tank gun, twenty-one anti-tank rifles, fifty machine guns and five trucks were destroyed or captured.

The Oak Leaves for Peiper

Operating afar, in the Soviet rear areas, Peiper's *Kampfgruppe* was able to eliminate a large number of strongpoints and prevented the enemy from establishing a bridgehead on the Teterew River. For this action and for the previous successes on the Ukrainian front, Peiper was awarded the Knight's Cross with Oak Leaves on 27 January 1944, as *Sturmbannführer und Kommandeur* of *SS-Pz.Rgt.1* of *"LSSAH"*. All of this, despite the heavy losses suffered by his tank units as a direct consequence of his actions that were overly foolhardy and audacious.

A photo of Peiper with the Oak Leaves "retouched".

An official photo of SS-Ostubaf. Jochen Peiper with the Knight's Cross with Oak Leaves.

Following is the citation written by *SS-Obf.* Wisch: "…*On 4 December 1943, the Division had been assigned the mission, beginning from the sector to the northeast of Tschernjachoff, along the line Mokrentschina-Pekartschina, on the flank and to the front of* XII.Armee-Korps, *to strike with energy and to wipe out the enemy forces, to subsequently enable, along with the other divisions of* XXXXVIII.Pz-Korps *and of the* XIII.Armee-Korps *to move towards the Teterew and establish contact with the* LIX.Armee-Korps. *Kampfgruppe Peiper, consisting of* SS-Pz.Rgt.1, SS-Pz.Aufkl.Abt.1, III.(gep.)/SS-Pz.Gr.Rgt.2, 2.SS-Pz.Pi.Btl.1 *and* 5.SS-Flak-Abt.1, *at 15:00 on on 5 December 1943 received orders to move, and after a night march to occupy Tschernjachoff, which is in enemy hands, then turn to the north of Tschernjachoff, make a wide swing to Andrejew, make it past the heights that surround Styrty and capture the sector of Radomyschl, without regard to any threat that might develop on the flank. After the* Kampfgruppe, *at 20:00 on 5 December, had reached the first hills of Sseljantschina, reconnaissance by* III.(gep.)/SS-Pz.Gr.Rgt.2 *had revealed that the enemy had developed extensive defensive positons distributed in depth, both to the west of Pekartschina as well as in the village itself. It was not possible to bypass the place, because of the particular nature of the terrain, but the bridge near the village had fallen undamaged into our hands.* SS-Sturmbannführer *Peiper, leading a battalion which had recently come under his command, during the night led it in an attack against that village with incredible courage. The enemy, taken completely by surprise in his positions in front of the village, was completely scattered by small arms and by flamethrowers on the armored vehicles. With a subsequent reconnaissance towards Andrejew, which* SS-Sturmbannführer *Peiper conducted personally, important information was gathered necessary for the attack on the following day, where he participated with his entire combat group. The results of the nighttime reconnaissance enabled him, at twilight, to deploy his units, and in the morning, at 6:00 hours, following brief artillery preparatory fire, to go on the attack and to seize Andrejew, blocking the Tsernjachoff-Korosten railway line. At this point, the* Kampfgruppe *had transported several batteries to the area to the east of Andrejew and after having destroyed several anti-tank guns and enemy strongpoints, captured the two hills around Styrty and around 10:00 hours, was able to report that it had reached the first objective. With an impetuous advance to the east, the* Kampfgruppe *clashed with and overran the first-line enemy artillery batteries and during the advance wiped out the combat positions of the 121st Rifle Division at Kisselowka, of the 322nd at Selizschy, of the 148th at Kamenny Brid and of the 336th at Kaitanowka. In this last locality the SS troops were able to resupply. In these days the* Kampfgruppe *captured or destroyed: 22 guns, 76 anti-tank guns, 38 anti-tank rifles, 49 machine guns, 40 vehicles, and 71 trucks. With*

A column of PzKpfw IV on the Ukrainian front, December 1943.

A PzKpfw IV and its crew.

Leibstandarte Panthers on the move, December 1943. (Charles Trang collection)

this strike, carried out over very difficult terrain, the Kampfgruppe *penetrated to a depth of thirty kilometers into enemy lines. Across the entire front, the divisions of* XIII.Armee-Korps *advanced contemporaneously, causing the enemy front to waver. Because the enemy, on 6 December, had temporarily cut the supply line, a platoon from the* Kampfgruppe, *on the afternoon of 7 December, advanced in the eastern sector deploying in front of Tschaikowka. This location had been rapidly reinforced by the Soviets who had also positioned numerous anti-tank guns on the ground, which caused losses.*

At dusk, SS-Sturmbannführer Peiper decided to halt the attack and to shift his troops to the north to hit Tschaikowka from the east. Around 19:00 the group was behind the enemy and after having hit the anti-tank positions, continued the advance for about ten kilometers. Soon after, however, the Kampfgruppe *was stopped by an order from the division, which had shifted its advance to the north. In the new attack direction, the* Kampfgruppe *seized the position at Chodory and then entered Sabolot, even though it was well defended. After this tough encounter in the field, which ended around 10:00 the following morning, SS-Sturmbannführer Peiper had the entire sector in his hands. In this night of battle,* Kampfgruppe Peiper *had captured or destroyed: one T-34 tank, one 4.5cm anti-tank gun, 61 7.62cm anti-tank guns, 21 anti-tank rifles, 55 machine guns, 5 vehicles…With this night advance inside the enemy lines, the* Kampfgruppe *had again operated in depth behind the enemy. SS-Sturmbannführer Peiper, in penetrating the enemy defensive system, had eliminated an important Soviet strongpoint and had opened a breach that enabled an enemy bridgehead on the Teterew to be broken and its formation prevented. SS-Sturmbannführer Peiper, in these days of combat, demonstrated high personal valor, just as he had demonstrated possession of an extraordinary sense of tactical command over his strong group. His personal courage, his combat plan, along with its decisive execution, as well as his ability to quickly assess situations and to capitalize on events, allowed his*

German grenadiers and Panthers on the Ukrainian front.

Theodor Wisch and Peiper discussing the situation.

A Soviet anti-tank position with a ZIS-3 gun.

SS-Obf. Wisch and SS-Stubaf. Lehmann.

Kampfgruppe and the entire division to achieve a major success. In a brief space of time, that runs from 21 November to 24 December 1943, SS-Pz.Rgt.1, under command of SS-Sturmbannführer Peiper, captured or destroyed a total as follows:100 T-34 tanks, 11 guns, 124 76.2cm Pak, 24 anti-tank rifles, 16 motor vehicles, 14 tractors, 7 anti-aircraft guns and two aircraft (LI-2). SS-Sturmbannführer Peiper has been under my command for a long time, and has always given proof of high personal valor and an extraordinary sense of command of his Regiment. I thus deem him to be worthy to receive the Oak Leaves for the Knight's Cross of the Iron Cross..."

Moving forward again

On 8 December, the units of the *Leibstandarte* resumed their advance in the northern sector and northwest of Radomyschl; the Soviets resisted stubbornly, forcing the SS troops to dig into defensive positions. The next day, due to the strong Soviet resistance, the attack northwest of Radomyschl was suspended and it was decided to send *SS-Pz.Gr.Rgt.2* and Peiper's *Panzerkampfgruppe* to the east, towards Mersheritschka and the Teterew, to try to cut off the Soviet troops defending Radomyschl.

This new action caught the Soviets by surprise and enabled the *Waffen SS* units to quickly reach the area northwest of Meshiritschka.

From the headquarters of XLVIII.Pz.Korps the order was given to the *Leibstandarte* to "...*assemble all available forces in the sector located southeast of Medelewka, so that the entire division, employing its artillery, its* Werfers, *its* Flak, *its panzers and its assault guns, could break through the enemy bridgehead in force from the north and then capture Meshiritschka*".

In the late afternoon, the forward elements of the division attacked Meshiritschka and half an hour later the Soviets were thrown back as far as the northern bank of the Teterew. At the same time, elements of the *68.Inf. Div.*, attacking from the south and from the west, had been able to break into Radomyschl. At dawn on 10 December, the *Leibstandarte* attacked towards Welikaja Rascha; the Soviet forces in the sector were well dug in and had strong artillery support. Peiper's tanks would suffer the consequences: around 8:00, the *Panzerkampfgruppe* moved from Meschiritschka towards Krasnoborki. Without having properly assessed the size of the enemy forces and the tactical situation, the SS tanks ended up under a terrific barrage fire, risking total annihilation. Facing that target shoot, *SS-Obf.* Wisch ordered an immediate suspension of the attack. Several hours later, Peiper attempted another frontal attack, incurring additional heavy losses. Wisch ordered Peiper to suspend any further offensive action and to withdraw. Deeply shaken by Peiper's lack of tactical sense, during the course of the night the commander of the *Leibstandarte* prepared an order relative to the proper employment of the units when conducting an attack, then having it distributed by Rudolph Lehmann to all unit commanders: a summary of methods and strategies that were known and had been tested in the field, drawn up for the express purpose of sensitizing his subordinates, Peiper in particular, to carry out attacks better and with fewer losses: "…*The attack across a vast plain, lacking any cover and against a well-organized defensive position, requires meticulous preparation of all of the movements of the infantry and armored units, with the support of the fire of all heavy weapons. In particular the preparatory fire of the artillery and* Nebelwerfer *batteries has to be exploited for an immediate advance forward.*

For this it is necessary to reach a good point of departure for the attack starting with the preparatory artillery fire. The attack must then develop according to the following phases:

Visual acquisition of the objective from the departure point so that it can be rapidly reached by armored and motorized units. Precise calculation of the time needed.

Employment of all officers in the front line. Emplace all of the 88mm guns as well as all medium-caliber Flak guns to combat the anti-tank guns on the flanks and to cover the flanks. Accurate targeting of all objectives by all of the heavy weapons, artillery and Nebelwerfer.

The armored group (panzers, assault guns, SPW and self-propelled artillery) must move to the departure point en bloc *and as soon as possible. From there, launch smoke rockets to mask the attack. The infantry must disperse widely; the artillery and heavy weapons must support them by opening fire on enemy anti-tank guns which have already been identified.*

Supporting fire by the artillery and Nebelwerfer *batteries; immediate breakthrough by the armored group,*

A *Leibstandarte Nebelwerfer* battery on the Ukrainian front. In the foreground is an MG-34 providing protection.

Leibstandarte grenadiers and half-track in combat.

A German armored unit on the Ukrainian front, December 1943.

41

German grenadiers and tanks attack on the Ukrainian front, December 1943.

Theodor Wisch (BDC)

A Tiger tank hits a T-34.

Peiper, with fur coat, along with other *Leibstandarte* officers.

in two phases: in the first, deep penetration. In the second, annihilation of enemy defenses with the coordinated employment of SPW and grenadiers, as well as by the infantry, which will follow on foot".

The *XLVIII.Pz.Korps* sent units of the *1.Pz.Div.* to the aid of the *Leibstandarte*; the army tank units attacked Krasnoborki from the north. On 11 December 1943, the SS units regrouped for the new attack against Krasnoborki, with the *I.* and *II./2* in the first echelon, *SS-StuG.-Abt.1* to the right of *I./2* and the *Panzerkampfgruppe* (*SS-Pz. Rgt.1* and *III.(gep.)/2*) to the left of *II./2*. At 11:55, all of the heavy weapons opened fire on the eastern portion of Krasnoborki; after only five minutes, the assault group attacked. At 12:50, thanks to support fire from the assault guns, the SS grenadiers broke into the town, engaging in bitter clashes in the streets, while Peiper's *Panzerkampfgruppe* continued on to the southeast. At 13:50, Peiper's group seized Hill 170 and the surrounding woods, destroying numerous enemy anti-tank positions.

At 15:00, *SS-Pz.Gr.Rgt.2* advanced as far as Welikaja Ratscha. At 16:50, the village was successfully attacked by the *Panzergruppe*. The next day, units of the *Leibstandarte* and of the *1.Pz.Div.* were engaged in wiping out Soviet forces located west of the Teterew. Around mid-December 1943, Peiper's tank regiment had only about a dozen operational tanks and, even more worrisome, many of his tank commanders had fallen in combat.

Once the offensive against Radomyschl had come to a close, there still remained to eliminate a solid Soviet bridgehead between the Teterew and Irscha rivers, in the Malin-Wischewitschi sector, where the remainder of the Soviet 60th Army was located. The *1.Pz.Div.* and the *Leibstandarte* were to attack along the Radomyschl-Sarudja road and take Iskra. On 14

Peiper congratulating Wittmann and members of his crew.

December, at 11:30, the *Panzergruppe* went on the attack; the position at Iskra was captured shortly after noontime. The panzers reached the Weprin-Federowka road, where the Soviets had established solid defensive positions. Avoiding a frontal attack, *SS-Stubaf.* Peiper made his armored group advance to the west, reaching the crossroads south of the eastern part of Fedorowka, where there were some enemy tanks. In the ensuing encounter, three enemy tanks were destroyed, but two SS tanks were also lost. Once the enemy bridgehead had been eliminated, the two German armored divisions were transferred to another sector.

In the weeks that followed, the *Leibstandarte* was engaged in defending the Berditchev-Katerinivka-Trayanov line. In early January 1944, many Soviet attacks were repulsed. The Tiger tanks were particularly engaged in the fighting, which always ensured a massive fire support during the defensive battles. On 5 January 1944, some forty Soviet tanks reached the area of Sherebin, behind the German lines. The *Leibstandarte* tanks and the *Luftwaffe* quickly joined the fray and within a few minutes, the enemy tanks were destroyed. *SS-Stubaf.* Peiper received special recognition by General Hermann Balck, commander of *XLVIII.Pz.Korps*, for the defensive successes of his *Panzer Regiment*. On 14 January 1944, *SS-Stubaf.* Peiper was present for the award of the *Ritterkreuz* to *SS-Ustuf.* Michael Wittmann, *Zugführer* (platoon leader) in the *13.(schw.)/SS-Pz.Rgt.1 "LSSAH"*,

January 1944: Peiper personally receiving the Oak Leaves from Hitler.

Witmann on the left, Peiper and other SS officers.

who with his Tiger had inflicted heavy losses upon Soviet armored formations.

On 20 January 12944, Peiper left the Eastern Front for a period of rest, as he was ill and needed treatment. The command of what was left of *SS-Pz.Rgt.1* passed to *SS-Stubaf*. Kuhlmann. On 27 January, on the occasion of the awarding of the Oak Leaves for his Knight's Cross, Peiper received a telegram from the *Führer*, which was also published in many papers at the time: "*In great recognition of your heroic actions in the fight for the future of our people, I confer the Knight's Cross with Oak Leaves as the 377th member awardee of the German armed forces. Adolf Hitler*".

The award was personally conferred by Hitler at his headquarters at Rastenburg in East Prussia. On 30 January 1944, Joachim Peiper was promoted to the rank of *SS-Obsrsturmbannführer*. A few days later, given a thorough medical exam, the doctors found numerous health problems in addition to extreme stress, and thus prescribed an extended convalescence so that he could regain his strength. Peiper took advantage of that to rest himself and to spend some time with his family.

On the Normandy front

The transfer of units of the *Leibstandarte* from the Eastern Front to the Western Front, in Belgium, was not completed until May 1944. The division had to be reorganized, but most of all there was fear of an Allied invasion along the French coast. *SS-Ostubaf.* Peiper, not yet completely healed, returned to his unit, in the Hasselt area, in late April, to take part in its reorganization and training of the new recruits. The new tanks arrived after much delay and the crews were busy training as simple infantrymen. The Tiger company was detached from the regiment in order to form an independent heavy tank battalion within the *SS-Pz. Korps*, and some of the best tankers in the division, such as Witmann, Woll and Staudegger, were transferred. It was thus necessary to designate new company commanders and new headquarters officers. The loss of the Tiger company was compensated in part by a new

SS-Ostubaf. Joachim Peiper.

Hasselt, Flanders, May 1944: SS-Ostubaf. Peiper inspects new recruits for his unit, which is reorganizing. In the photo on the left, SS-Ustuf. Kurt Köchlin, his aide is next to him.(Ordonnanz Offizier)

Conferring awards to members of SS-Pz.Rgt.1.

Hasselt, Flanders, May 1944: Peiper inspecting new recruits.

Flanders, May 1944: Peiper during a unit inspection ceremony. In the photo on the right is SS-Ostubaf. Frey.

Belgium, May 1944: On the left is Peiper's Befehlpanzer IV with two members of its crew, SS-Uscha. Otto Becker and Fritz Kosmehl. In the photo to the right, a PzKpfw IV of 7.Kp./SS-Pz.Rgt.1 during training.

June 1944: Panthers of SS-Pz.Rgt.1 in a Belgian town.

supply company, the *Versorgungs-Kompanie*, to ensure the regiment greater independence. The headquarters companies were reinforced with a reconnaissance platoon, a *Flak* platoon consisting of three 20mm *Flakvierling* on SdKfz.8/2 vehicles, a motorcycle platoon and an engineer platoon. The *I.Abteilung* continued to be equipped with Panther tanks, but each of the companies lost a platoon of five vehicles compared to the earlier issue, so that the number of tanks per company fell from twenty-two to seventeen. Overall, the battalion was supposed to have seventy-three Panthers, including the five assigned to its headquarters company. The *II.Abteilung*, remained equipped with the PzKpfw IV, twenty-two per company and eight in its headquarters company. The regimental headquarters company was also equipped with PzKpfw IV tanks; Jochem Peiper's tank bore *turmnummer* "001".

On 6 June 1944, the Allies landed in Normandy and the *Leibstandarte* was put on alert. The leaders of the OKW were, however, convinced that the landings were only a diversion and that the real landings would take place in the Pas de Calais area, so on 9 June the division was ordered to move to the region to the east of Bruges. On 12 June, after Hitler became convinced that the main landing was

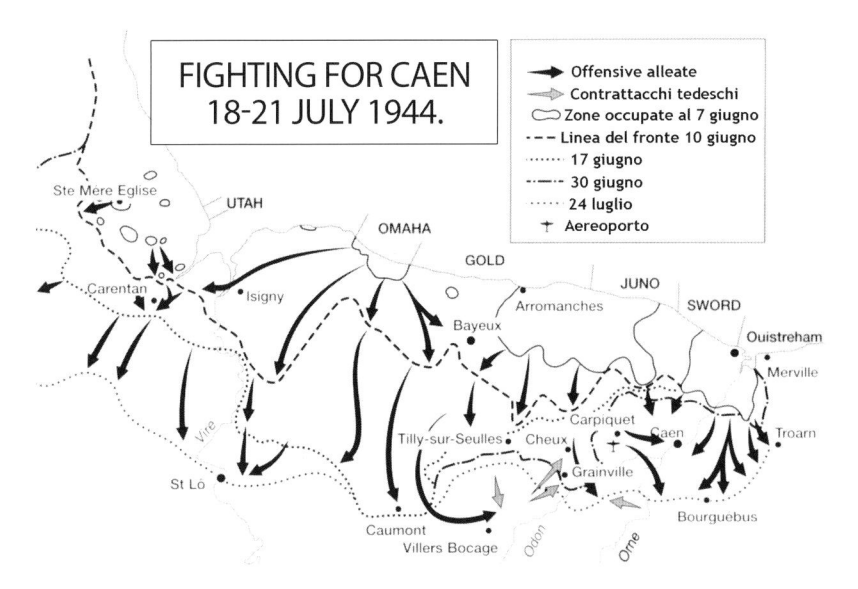

Situation on the Normandy front between June and July 1944.

A Pz.IV of the LSSAH in Normandy.

A Waffen SS Panther on the Normandy front, July 1944.

A Panther rolls past a defensive position with an MG-42.

47

FIGHTING FOR CAEN 18-21 JULY 1944

A Waffen SS Panther in Normandy. (NA)

A Panther tank moving to attack.

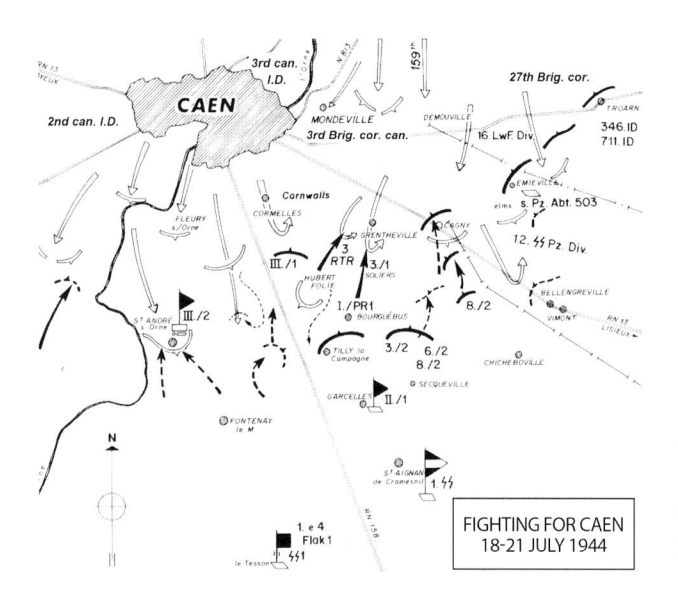

SS-Ostuf. Hans Malkones (BDC)

indeed in Normandy, the *Leibstandarte* was ordered to be transferred immediately to the *I.SS-Pz.Korps* in the Caen area, where the *12.SS-Pz.Div. "Hitlerjugend"* was already fighting. However, left behind in Belgium were some of the infantry units, the tank crews that had not yet received their vehicles, and elements of the reconnaissance group and of the artillery regiment. Peiper's first armored units did not reach Caen until 5 July 1944; a few days later, units of the *"Hitlerjugend"* withdrew across the Orne River, abandoning Caen to the Allies. *SS-Ostubaf.* Peiper was ordered to detach his *II.Abteilung* to the *II.SS-Panzer-Korps* right sector. On 11 July, the *Leibstandarte* occupied the area to the south of Caen, with Maltot to the west and the Caen-Falaise road to the east. The remaining Panthers of Peiper's *I.Abteilung* were positioned to the rear, as corps reserve. Beginning on 15 July, the *Leibstandarte* units moved to both sides of road RN 158, between Ifs and Cintheaux. *SS-Pz.Rgt.1*, commanded by *SS-Stubaf.* Kuhlmann, assumed positions to the east of RN 158; the Panther tanks were camouflaged in the woods in order to avoid being spotted by enemy aircraft, which were always lurking nearby.

On 16 July, the *2.Zug* (2nd Platoon) of *5.Kp./SS-Pz. Rgt.1*, commanded by *SS-Ustuf.* Günter Pflughaupt, had to support the attack of the *9.SS-Pz.Div. "Hohenstaufen"* against Baron and Hill 112. Within a few minutes, four of the platoon's PzKpfw IV tanks were knocked out during the attack against the hill. All of the tank commanders and most of the crews were captured by the enemy.

July 1944: The commander of a LSSAH Panther scanning the horizon. (Michael Cremin collection).

A Panther on the Normandy front, July 1944.

An MG-42 and a Waffen-SS Panther. (Münchner ill.Press)

Operation Goodwood

On 18 July 1944, the Allies launched Operation "Goodwood", a major offensive in the region to the east of the Orne River. The operation was preceded by a massive Allied artillery and air bombardment. Marshal Bernard Law Montgomery had assembled five infantry divisions, three armored divisions and another three armored brigades, with a total of more than a thousand tanks. The objective was to fix and destroy the German armored formations and to open the road to Falaise. General Heinrich Eberbach, the new commander of *Panzergruppe West*, guessed the Allied intentions and ordered *SS-Ogruf.* Dietrich to mount an immediate counterattack in the Bourgebus area with his reserves. Soon after, the order was transmitted to Peiper, with the remnants of his *Panzer-Regiment* in reserve. He consulted with *SS-Ostubaf.* Max Wünsche, commander of *SS-Pz.Rgt.12*, to plan the operation. In contrast to what had happened on the Eastern Front, Peiper did not personally participate in the front-line fighting.

The I./SS-Pz.Rgt.1, with a strength of forty-six Panther tanks, was to counterattack from the area to the east of Rocquancourt to push the British to the other side of the Caen-Troarn railway line. *SS-Stubaf.* Heinz Kling was to provide fire support on the flanks, with the available elements of *II./SS-Pz.Rgt.1* and of *SS-StuG.Abt.1*. Allied aviation did not spot the movements of *SS-Panzer-Regiment 1*; around noon, Peiper ordered Kuhlmann to move from the southeast to the area to the east of Bourguebus. He advanced in battle formation, preceded by SS half-tracks. As soon as the two units crested the ridge straddling Bourguebus, they were faced by a British armored regiment, the Fife and Forfar Yeomanry. In the encounter that followed, the British lost 29 tanks and their commander, within the

A LSSAH PzKpfw IV.

Command tank (Befehlswagen) "R02" of the LSSAH in Normandy, summer 1944.

space of a few minutes. Kuhlmann then ordered his unit to resume the advance immediately. The *2.Kp./SS-Pz. Rgt.1*, led by *SS-Ostuf.* Hans Malkomes, distinguished itself particularly in this action; after having received the order to engage the enemy tanks in the Soliers area, his thirteen Panthers moved quickly towards Bourguebus. An enemy force was then intercepted consisting of some sixty tanks to the south and southeast of Soliers, while another twenty or so enemy tanks had hidden themselves well in the Norman bocage. Despite their inferior numbers, the SS Panthers went on the attack; exploiting the surprise factor, at least twenty enemy tanks were destroyed while at the same time the position at Soliers was being attacked. The British attacks resumed on 19 July. All of the British armored divisions were committed to combat. The *Leibstandarte* continued to defend its positions. The SS grenadiers and the *7.Kp.* with its PzKpfw IV tanks had taken up defensive positions in the Tilly-la-Campagne area. The *Leibstandarte* Panthers were deployed in the area to the east of Bourguebus. An

SS-Ostuf. Werner Sternebeck.

SS-Ostubaf. Joachim Peiper.

SS-Stubaf. Herbert Kuhlmann (BDC).

SS-Stubaf. Werner Peoetschke.

enemy attack against Tilly-la-Campagne was driven back after bitter fighting. The village remained in German hands. At the same time, the 5th Royal Tank Regiment advanced on both sides of Bourguebus, ending up under fire from the *Leibstandarte's* panzers and 88mm *Flak* guns. After having lost eight Sherman tanks, the British were forced to withdraw. On 20 July as well, Peiper's tanks continued to be engaged in furious fighting.

The tanks of the *5.* and *6.Pz.Kp.* were able to conduct a successful counterattack. The next day, the *Leibstandarte* Panthers advanced along Route Nationale 158; the Panthers managed to pass through the enemy positions, getting as far as the outskirts of Ifs. Shortly after, however, having come under heavy fire from enemy tanks and artillery, they had to withdraw. That same day, Montgomery was forced to suspend Operation "Goodwind", not having achieved any of the planned objectives.

Operation "Spring"

On 25 July 1944, the Allies launched Operation "Spring"; according to Montgomery's plans, four Canadian and British divisions were to seize the area of Fontenay le Marmion-Garcelles, defended by units of the *Leibstandarte*. When the operation began, Peiper's *Panzer Regiment* had 41 operational PzKpfw IV tanks. The *7.Pz.Kp.* under *SS-Ostuf.* Werner Wolff was still in the Tilly-la-Campagne area, while the other three companies of *II.Pz.Abteilung* were kept in reserve. Additionally, Peiper had once again to detach his *I.Pz. Abteilung*, this time to *SS-Pz.Rgt.12*. During the night, the Canadian 3rd Infantry Division launched an attack against the *Leibstandarte's* left flank, in the Tilly-la-Campagne area. The attack was thrown back with heavy losses. The SS grenadiers and the tankers were engaged in furious close-quarter combat, using hand grenades and machine pistols. The Tilly-la-Campagne position continued to be the scene of tough fighting until the SS units were relieved on 5 August.

Meanwhile, in the area to the west of the Caen-Falaise road, the bulk of the *Leibstandarte* was preparing to rebuff the attack of the Canadian 2nd Infantry Division. Particularly pressed in the fighting that followed was the *5.Kp./ SS-Pz.Rgt.1*, led by *SS-Ostuf.* Werner Sternebeck, which was able to temporarily stall the enemy attack. In fact, soon after, the Canadian units, under cover of a thick artificial fog, were able to pass through the positions defended by the *Panzer SS*. At that point, Sternebeck was forced to order his tanks to pull back; during the withdrawal his second platoon and the headquarters platoon came under fire from Canadian anti-tank guns located at Troteval.

51

Rhaden, November 1944: Peiper during a ceremony honoring the 1923 Putsch.

Peiper presenting awards to his men.

Four PzKpfw IV, including Sternebeck's, were knocked out in the fighting, while the rest of the tanks of *5.Kp./ SS-Pz.Rgt.1* were engaged unsuccessfully in defending the position at Verriéres, where *1.Kp.* and *15.Kp.* of *SS-Pz.Gr.Rgt.1* were fighting, along with a few assault guns of *1.Bttr./SS-StuG.-Abt.1*. *SS-Oscha.* Theo Jensen, with two PzKpfw IV, launched a desperate counterattack to prevent the Canadian troops from exploiting their breakthrough. His tank came under enemy fire and was badly damaged. *SS-Oscha.* Jensen, however, managed to come out alive; after being captured, he was killed in cold blood by a Canadian officer. Capitalizing upon this success, the 1st Royal Tank Regiment, with infantry support, moved towards Rocquancourt; at about four hundred meters south of Verriéres, it was halted by fire from the heavy weapons of *I./SS-Pz.Gr.Rgt.*1, by the assault guns of *SS-StuG.-Abt.1* and by the Panthers of *I./SS-Pz.Rgt. 9* of the "*Hohenstaufen*". At least eight Cromwell tanks were knocked out during this defensive battle.

On 2 August 1944, *SS-Ostubaf.* Joachim Peiper was sent urgently to hospital due to a sudden gallbladder attack, coupled with a sudden nervous crisis, so that *SS-Stubaf.* Herbert Kuhlmann assumed command of *SS-Pz.Rgt.1.* while command of *I./SS-Pz.Rgt.*1 was passed to *SS-Hstuf.* Werner Poetschke. In early September 1944 Peiper was sent to the military hospital near Tegernsee, in northern Bavaria, not far from his family. He convalesced until 7 October.

Reorganization of the armored regiment

The remnants of the *Leibstandarte Panzer-Regiment* were concentrated first at Chantilly, north of Paris, then to be transferred to Hasselt in Belgium. On 4 September 1944, the remnants of all of the *Leibstandarte* were sent back to Germany to be reorganized, in the Siegburg area; among the first units to reach the new assembly area were what was left of *SS-Pz. Rgt.1.* The surviving elements of the *I.Abteilung* found themselves dispersed between the towns of Dellbrück, Holweide and Brück, near Cologne, while those of *II.Abteilung* were scattered through the villages of Birk, Geber and Bergisch. The *Leibstandarte* armored unit had temporarily come under the command of *SS-Hstuf.* Poetschke, while awaiting Peiper's return. At the beginning of October, the *Leibstandarte* left the Siegburg area, to be moved to the eastern part of Westphalia; the divisional headquarters was installed in Lubeck. The reorganization of the units proceeded apace, but men and equipment were lacking. In particular, the new recruits who were earmarked to form the new tank crews had never set foot in a tank. Lacking the complete issue of tanks called for, *SS-Pz.Rgt.1* was completely reorganized by Peiper: during October 1944 the headquarters, headquarters company, and the *1.* and *2.Kp.* of *I.Abteilung* were transferred to Wietzendorf, in the Münsterlager complex. Shortly thereafter, the *6.* and *7.Kp.* of *II.Abteilung* also arrived. Poetschke's *I.Abteilung* now included only two companies, the *1.*and *2.*, equipped with PzKpfw V Panther tanks and two companies equipped with PzKpfw IV, the *6.* and *7. Kp.*

All of the available tanks were concentrated in this mixed battalion, while *II.Abteilung* sought to gather together all of the crews still without tanks, from companies *3., 4., 5.* and *8*. In order to provide adequate air defense protection to the SS tank units, the motorized *10.(Flak).Kp.* was organized, commanded by *SS-Ostuf.* Karl-Heinz Vögler, consisting of two platoons, each equipped with two *Flakpanzer IV "Wirbelwind"* and two *Flakpanzer IV "Ostwind"* and a platoon of *Flakvierling* (quad 20mm *Flak* guns).

Offensive in the Ardennes

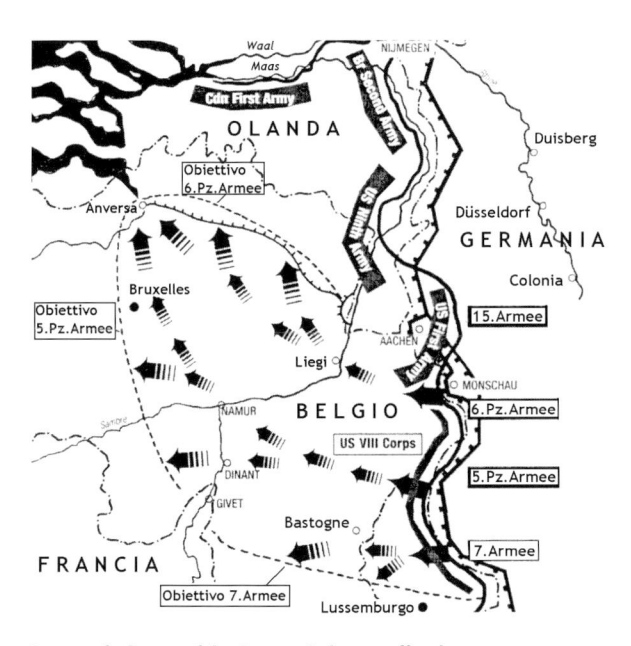

Routes of advance of the German Ardennes offensive.

Official historiography remembers Jochen Peiper above all for his participation in the German offensive in the Ardennes in late 1944, and in particular for his involvement in the massacre of American prisoners at Malmedy. *SS-Ostubaf.* Peiper, leading his armored group, did not accomplish his mission, but his action caused so much fear and so much worry in the Allied command hierarchy that it became one of the episodes of the Second World War that has been exhaustively covered by military history experts, in addition to being to this day one of the actions of the war that is most studied in military schools and academies throughout the world.

Operation "Autumn Fog"

Operation *Herbstnebel* (Autumn Fog), the final name given to the new German offensive in the Ardennes, called for the attack by fully three armies, the *6.Panzerarmee* (Dietrich) in the north, the *5.Panzerarmeee* (von Manteuffel) in the center and the *7.Armee* (Brandenberger) in the south, crossing through the Ardennes between Aachen and Luxembourg. The primary objective was to reach the River Meuse, and the secondary, further objective was Anvers. The general plan called for breaking through the Allied lines in the Ardennes with the aim of separating the American forces, deployed in France, from the British, deployed in Belgium and Holland, and to capture Anvers and its port in order to stop the flow of Allied supplies. The orders for the *6.Panzerarmee* were to

SS-Obstgruf. Sepp Dietrich, December 1944.

SS-Ostubaf. Peiper in Westphalia, November 1944.

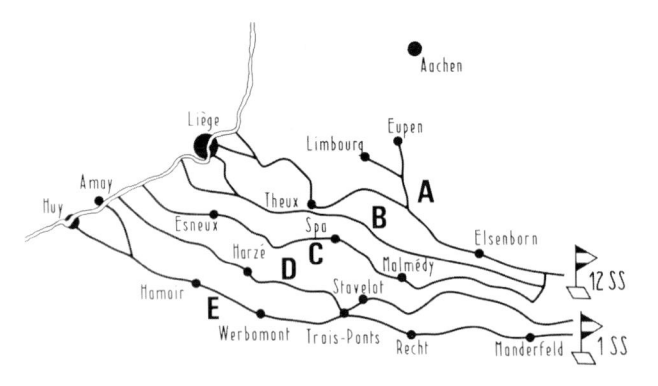

Attack routes of the two divisions of *I.SS-Pz.Korps* planned for the offensive.

Men of *SS-Panzer-Brigade 150* on the eve of the offensive.

A *Waffen-SS* motorized column on the move, December 1944.

SS-Ostubaf. Otto Skorzeny.

break through the American front north of the Schnee Eifel, a heavily forested area along the German-Belgian border and to aim for the Meuse, which was to be crossed between Liege and Huy. Tactically, it had been decided to use infantry units to make the initial penetration of the enemy lines, while the armored units would join the action soon after in order to exploit the gaps that had been opened. The *SS-Pz.Korps*, commanded by *SS-Ogruf.* Hermann Priess, was to play a fundamental role: his mission was to break through the American lines between Hollerath and Krewinkel, with the *227. Volksgrenadier-Division*, the *12.Volksgrenadier-Division* and the *3.Fallschirmjäger-Division*. Their breakthrough was to be followed up quickly by units of *12.SS-Pz.Div. "Hitlerjugend"*, to which routes of attack A, B and C (thus identified on maps) had been assigned and by *the 1.SS-Pz.Div."Leibstandarte"*, which had been put under command of *SS-Oberführer* Wilhelm Monke, along attack axes D and E. Along attack axis D, behind *SS-Kampgruppe Peiper*, which constituted the *Leibstandarte's* spearhead, *Kampfgruppe Sandig* was supposed to follow, led by *SS-Ostubaf.* Rudolf Sandig, commander of *SS-Pz.Gr.Rgt.2*, in turn followed by the headquarters of the *Leibstandarte* and of the *I.SS-Pz.Korps* itself. Along attack axis E. *Kampfgruppe Hansen*, led by *SS-Ostubaf.* Max Hansen, commander of *SS-Pz.Gr.Rgt.1*, was to take the lead, closely followed by *Kampfgruppe Knittel*, led by *SS-Stubaf.* Knittel, commander of *SS-Pz.Aufkl. Abt.1*. Sepp Dietrich's *6.Panzerarmee* was positioned on the left flank of the attack front and was to exert the greatest effort; the *I.SS-Pz.Korps* was to lead the advance to the Meuse, with *II.SS-Pz.Korps* following behind it, ready to join the action and exploit any breakthroughs.

Once crossings had been secured across the river, Bittrich's divisions were to become the spearhead of the advance to Anvers. In order assist Dietrich's units to reach the bridges before the Americans could blow them sky-high, Otto Skorzeny's Special Brigade, *SS-Panzer-Brigade 150*[9], with several squads of "fake" American soldiers, was

---

[9] When the armored spearheads of the *Leibstandarte* moved forward, Skorzeny's men followed in wheeled vehicles. However, the march was soon stalled by the traffic jams along the very few available roads. With Peiper's

to create panic and chaos within the enemy lines (Operation *Greif*), while a *Luftwaffe* parachute regiment under *Oberstleutnant* von der Heydte, was to be dropped past the Allied lines to seize several vital road junctions (Operation *Stösser*). The *Leibstandarte* and the *Hitlerjugend* were to advance side by side to the Meuse, after the *Volksgrenadier* divisions had opened the way through the weak American defenses along the Belgian-German border. Once the breach had been made, the two divisions were to move through the Ardennes forests until they had reached the valley of the Meuse. The roads throughout the region were very narrow and in some places only allowed a single-file column of vehicles to move; the roughly six thousand *Waffen-SS* vehicles would soon clog and jam the roads. The difficult road net also dictated that each division had only two routes available, so that the combat groups were forced to move one behind the other and wait for the forward troops to open the road. A final consideration was the problem of fuel; despite the fact that the German logistic services had managed to scrape together more than seventeen million liters of fuel for the offensive, the traffic jams prevented the supplies from reaching the armored spearheads with any regularity. *SS-Ostubaf.* Peiper and his *Kampfgruppe* were thus ordered to "loot" any Allied fuel dumps they ran across, in order to be able to continue their advance through the Ardennes.

Panzergruppe Peiper

The *Leibstandarte's* armored regiment had been reorganized with only one operational battalion, consisting of thirty-eight Panther tanks and thirty-four PzKpfw IV. In order to increase the division's armored

panzers stalled in the snarled traffic, some units abandoned the main roads to move across the open fields, then bogging down in the mud, or worse, ending up in the middle of minefields. The commander of *Kampfgruppe X, SS-Ostubaf.* Hardieck, was killed by a mine while with his men he was attempting to avoid a jam caused by an army unit. Command of the *Kampfgruppe* then passed to *SS-Hstuf.* Adrian von Voelkersam. Despite the traffic jams and the chaos, eight jeeps of *Einheit Steilau*, with the men in enemy uniforms, were able to insert themselves into the enemy lines and during the night of the 16th began to wander undisturbed in the Allied rear area, reaching as far as the Meuse. *SS-Hstuf.* Steileau's men had been organized into four special reconnaissance squads, two demolition squads and six "commando" squads, three of which were assigned to the *Panzerbrigade* and the other three assigned to the *Leibstandarte*, *Hitlerjugend* and *12.Volksgr.Div*. Skorzeny's "fake" Americans managed to interrupt traffic at several bridges on the Meuse, such as at Liege and Huy, diverting the movement of Allied troops. At the same time, a squad prevented the destruction of the bridge over the Amblève at Stavelot, allowing *Kampfgruppe Peiper's* vehicles to cross. At some particularly key intersections, some Germans in American uniforms and some even wearing the Military Police armbands, directed traffic after having moved the road signs; in this way, entire American units were diverted to the rear instead of reaching the front line. Then the actual sabotage began: an entire ammunition dump was blown up and telephone lines were cut everywhere. So many acts of sabotage were committed that total chaos ensued among the Allied forces.

The Tigers of *s.SS-Pz.Abt. 501* passing through Tondorf.

SS-Ostuf. Georg Preuss.

A Panther tank of *Kampfgruppe Peiper* passing a supply column.

German artillery opening fire against enemy positions.

German troops attacking on the Ardennes front. (NA)

strength, it was assigned the *Schwere SS-Pz.Abt.501*, formed from the old *s.SS-Pz.Abt.101*, consisting of about thirty *Königstiger* (King Tiger) tanks. On the eve of the Ardennes operation, *Panzergurppe Peiper*, or *SS Kampfgruppe Peiper*, consisted of the following units:

SS-Panzer-Regiment 1 (*SS-Ostubaf.* Jochen Peiper)
- I.*(gemischte)Kp.* (*SS-Stubaf.* Werner Poetschke)
- *Stab Kompanie I./SS-Pz.Rgt.1* (*SS-Ustuf.* Buchheim)
- *Nachschub Kompanie I./SS-Pz.Rgt.1* (*SS-Hstuf.* Otto)
- *1./SS-Pz.Rgt.1* (*SS-Ostuf.* Karl Kremser)
- *2./SS-Pz.Rgt.1* (*SS-Ostuf.* Friedrich Christ)
- *6./SS-Pz.Rgt.1* (*SS-Ostuf* Benoni Junker)
- *7./SS-Pz.Rgt.1* (*SS-Hstuf.* Oskar Klingelhöfer)
- *9.(Pi.)/SS-Pz.Rgt.1* (*SS-Ostuf.* Erich Rumpf)
- *10.(Flak)/SS-Pz.Rgt.1* (*SS-Ostuf.* Karl-Heinz Vögler)
- *Instandsetz.Kp./SS-Pz.Rgt.1* (*SS-Ostuf.* Ratschko)

Schw.SS-PanzerAbt.501 (*SS-Ostubaf.* von Westernhagen)
- *Nachschub Kompanie* (*SS-Ostuf.* Paul Vogt)
- *1./Kp.* (*SS-Ostuf.* Jürgen Wessel)
- *2./Kp.* (*SS-Hstuf.* Rolf Möbius)
- *3./Kp.* (*SS-Hstuf.* Heinz Birnschein)
- *4.(leichte)Kp.* (*SS-Hstuf.* Wilhelm Spitz)

III.(gep.)/SS-Panzer-Gren.-Rgt.2 (*SS-Hstuf.* Diefenthal)
- *9.(gep.)Kp.* (*SS-Ustuf.* Max Leike)
- *10(gep.)Kp.* (*SS-Ostuf.* Georg Preuss)
- *11.(gep.)Kp.* (*SS-Ostuf.* Heinz Tomhardt)
- *12(gep.)Kp.* (*SS-Hscha.* Jochen Thiele)
- *Nachschub Kp. III(gep.)/2* (*SS-Ostuf.* Lüdecke)

Other attached units
- *13.(IG.0/SS-Pz.Gr.Rgt.2* (*SS-Ostuf.* Koch)
- *3.(gep.)/SS-Pz.Pi.Btl.1* (*SS-Ostuf.* Franz Sievers)
- *Flak-Abteilung 84* (*Luftwaffe*) (*Major* von Sacken)

The *Leibstandarte* units reached their assembly area in the forest of Blankenheim. On the morning of 14 December, *SS-Ostubaf.* Peiper was informed by the division headquarters of the role his *Kampfgruppe* was to play: his armored group would be the division's spearhead. Meetings with his officers followed to discuss the most minute details of their planned actions. Among the chief missions to be carried out was that of

SS-Ostubaf. Peiper.

Vehicles crossing over a hasty bridge built by German engineers.

SS-Obf. Mohnke stopped with his vehicle along the road.

A column of PzKpfw IV and half-tracks on the move, December 1944.

making contact with *Kampfgruppe X*, commanded by *SS-Ostubaf.*

Willi Hardieck of *Panzer Brigade 150*. The march order was also established: the vanguard of the *Kampfgruppe*, the so-called *spitze* (literally, the "head" or "top"), led by *SS-Ostuf.* Werner Sternebeck, consisted of a platoon of five PzKpfw IV of the *6./SS-Pz.Rgt.1*, a half platoon of two Panthers from *1.Kompanie* and an engineer squad from *9.Kompanie*. Immediately behind was the *Spitzen Kompanie* led by *SS-Hstuf.* Georg Preuss, consisting of his *10.Kp./SS-Pz.Gren. Rgt.2*, an engineer platoon from *9.Kp./SS-Pz.Rgt.1* and a heavy weapons platoon from *12.Kp./SS-Pz.Gren. Rgt.2*. The rest of the *Kampfgruppe* then followed, formed by the other units of *SS-Pz.Rgt.1* and *SS-Pz. Gren.Rgt.2* and finally the *Schwere SS-Panzer Abteilung 501* and the *Luftwaffe Flak* battalion. Peiper calculated that the entire march column would be at least twenty-five kilometers long and that it would take at least two hours before the column could clear any particular point.

The offensive kicks off

At 5:30 on 16 December 1944, artillery and *Nebelwerfer* batteries unleashed an inferno of fire on the American positions along the Belgian-German border. In truth, the German barrage did not last long nor did it cause many casualties to the Allied units; around 7:00, the first wave of German infantry units attacked to open the way for the armored columns. Units of the *12.Volksgrenadier-Division* and of the *3.Fallschirmjäger-Division* soon ran into stiff resistance. Their objective was to capture the city of Losheim and its road junctions in a few hours in order to enable the tanks of Peiper's *Kampfgruppe* to go into action during the morning. However, the presence of extensive minefields slowed down the progress of the German units and the two divisions were still fighting to open a gap between the American positions when *SS-Ostubaf.* Peiper, at 8:00, positioned his units immediately behind the operational area of the *12.Volksgrenadier-Division*. It was only after bitter fighting that the *Volksgrenadieren* were able to take Losheim. The march of the units was still stalled because a stretch of railway line had to be crossed, which passed through a deep cut, and the road bridge that spanned it had been destroyed by the enemy. The *Kampfgruppe* engineers reported that it was not possible to repair the bridge before noontime. Peiper, determined not to lose all of that time, then ordered his engineers to partially fill the cut with dirt and other material so

57

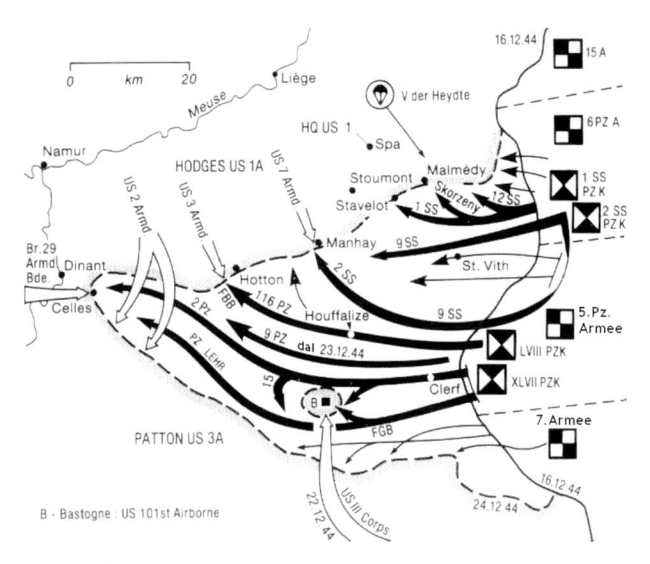

Routes of the German offensive with the dates and front line trace.

Fallschirmjäger examining an enemy submachine gun.

December 1944, German troops moving in the assault.

The 9th Regiment of the 3.Fallschirmjäger-Division had been stopped cold at Lanzerath and was reporting strong enemy resistance coming from the forest at Büllingen. This regiment was assigned to me and it was possible to advance again".

Continuing his advance, Peiper found the road along his attack route totally jammed by columns of other German units, mainly by armored columns, towed artillery and infantry on foot. Finding himself practically bottled up and desiring to press on ahead, after a brief talk with the commander of *12.Volksgrenadier-Division*, Peiper decided to modify his march route; it was a difficult but necessary choice, in order to complete his assigned mission. Finding the road blocked by artillery of the *12.Volksgrenadier-Division* and noticing that the army artillerymen did not move over to let him pass, Peiper ordered his men to move forward and to push the towed guns off the road. From his point of view, the mission that had been assigned to him was more important than a few artillery pieces and the horses pulling them. The forward elements of the *Kampfgruppe* reached Losheim in the morning; Peiper was ordered to move to the west and to support the attack of the *3.Fallschirmjäger-Division* against Honsfeld. The road to Lanzerath was mined; near Hüllscheid the *Kampfgruppe* ended up in a German minefield, where it lost two Panthers. But this did not stop Peiper, who ordered his men to continue to press forward. Southeast of Merlscheid the leading elements of the *Kampfgruppe*

that the advance could continue. Let us read Peiper's own account[10]: "...*Because crossing the railway line had not yet been completed, my group descended from the edge of the railway embankment and, guided by necessity, crossed the rocky gorge just a few meters from the railway bridge. Around dusk, the crossing was completed and we reached Losheimergraben, which was under fire by heavy artillery. There, I received the order over the telephone from army corps headquarters to no longer proceed along the planned attack route, but to turn to the west towards Lanzerath.*

---

[10] Interview granted by Peiper, 22 February 1959.

also ended up in a minefield, losing *SS-Ostuf.* Sternebeck's PzKpfw IV. *SS-Ostubaf.* Peiper reached Lanzerath around midnight, where he quickly met with the commander of *Fallschirmjäger-Regiment 9*, *Oberst* von Hoffmann, who reported that the forest at Büllingen heavily mined and occupied by large enemy forces. In reality, the parachute regiment had been hit by intense rifle fire on its flank, but no one had bothered to send out reconnaissance patrols to determine the positions and strength of the enemy units. The *Fallschirmjäger* were not in the least mindful of the urgency to move forward, nor did they seem ready to do so. Peiper thus decided to not attack at night without artillery support.

A tank commander leading the attack. (U.S.Army)

Kampfgruppe Peiper vehicles entering Honsfeld.

Half-tracks and grenadiers of *SS-Kampfgruppe Peiper* entering Honsfeld, 17 December 1944. (U.S. Army)

In addition, despite orders, Hoffmann refused to subordinate his regiment to Peiper, an officer whose rank was lower than his. The corps headquarters then ordered the *Oberst* to relinquish his *II.Bataillon*, led by Major Taubert, to *Kampfgruppe Peiper*.

And thus, on 17 December 1944, at 4:00 in the morning, Peiper made his attack against the forest of Büllingen, employing the *Fallschirmjäger* of *II./Fall. Rgt.9*. The *10.Kp./SS-Pz.Gr.Rgt.2* under *SS-Hstuf.* Preuss took the lead, because its SPW were faster and moved better through the wooded terrain, while Sternebeck's *Spitze* followed closely behind, with a company of paratroopers who had climbed aboard his tanks and with the other three *Fallschirmjäger* companies on foot. It soon became clear that there was no minefield and that there were no enemy defensive positions in the forest, as Peiper himself relates: "..*We entered into the woods without firing a shot, discovering that it was completely empty*". *SS-Ostubaf.* Peiper went into a raging fury over the useless waste of time. "…*There was neither enemy resistance nor mines in the woods. The paratroopers had in fact not attacked, preferring instead to remain in the warm billets in Lanzerath*".

Towards Honsfeld

Once the woods had been taken, Sternebeck's *Spitze* took the lead again, quickly making contact with some American units which immediately disappeared into the darkness without engaging in any fighting. The railway station at Losheimergraben, the station at Bucholz, immediately to the right of the *Kampfgruppe's* march route towards Honsfeld, was occupied by enemy forces, but this did not in any way interfere with the movement of the German units. After having bypassed it, *SS-Ostuf.* Sternebeck's Spitze continued its march towards Honsfeld. Following is his report[11]: "…*Around 4:30 we reached Honsfeld. Along the right side of the road in our direction of march, there was an armored column (tanks, armored cars, jeeps), a reconnaissance unit. I thought that his might be a unit of* Einsatzgruppe "Greif"[12]. *I stopped near the column to verify this. I climbed down from my panzer and jumped on another to look for the "Z" on the turret. Unfortunately, my search was in vain. We were in the midst of the enemy, who was asleep. My reaction was to climb aboard my panzer again and order a rapid retreat towards the northeastern exit of the village and to report the*

---

[11] Werner Sternebeck, report on the Ardennes offensive.
[12] The special units of Skorzeny's *SS-Panzerbrigade 150*.

A PzKpfw. V and a group of American prisoners.

A *Flakpanzer IV "Wirbelwind"* of the LAH at Honsfeld.

A Panther of *SS-Kampfgruppe Peiper* on the move.

SS soldiers collecting fuel in Honsfeld.

presence of the enemy to the armored battalion". *SS-Ostuf.* Sternebeck had thought that the vehicles were part of Skorzeny's special unit who were wandering about in enemy uniforms using enemy vehicles, but that was not the case. He then returned to Büllingen, leaving the capture of Honsfeld to other units of *Kampfgruppe Peiper*.

Around 6:00, the bulk of the *Kampfgruppe* reached Honsfeld, finding the American units still asleep, as Peiper himself tells us:"..*As soon as we entered Honsfeld at a steady speed at the first light of dawn, we awakened an American reconnaissance battalion. The anti-tank guns were destroyed; the streets, alleys and courtyards were full o armored vehicles, jeeps and tanks and we were looked at through the windows by the sleepy eyes of hundreds of speechless American soldiers. We continued to move on, firing a few machine gun bursts towards the houses and continued on towards Büllingen. It was our intention to let the paratroopers mop up the position, while a single company, which had climbed aboard the leading tanks, remained with the* Kampfgruppe *until the end of the offensive*".

It was not until after the bulk of the *Kampfgruppe* had crossed through the town that the Americans regained their balance, attacking the German paratroopers and tanks that followed; as a result, Panthers "232" and "235" were knocked out by fire from American anti-tank guns. During the firefights that followed, *SS-Ostuf.* Vögler, commander of *10.(Flak)Kp./SS-Pz.Rgt.1*, was wounded. In the end, it was the providential appearance of a Tiger II that forced the Americans to surrender; hit four times, the King Tiger continued to move forward, demolishing a wall and crushing two anti-tank guns under its tracks. At the end of the fighting, the *Kampfgruppe* salvaged about fifty armored and half-tracked vehicles, about eighty trucks and fifteen anti-tank guns, while the paratroopers found a fuel dump where the SS tanks

Fallschirmjäger following the *Kampfgruppe*, salvaging enemy material.

A bazooka in action (NA)

German soldiers taking boots from dead enemy soldiers at Honsfeld.

A German armored column moving in the Ardennes.

refueled. Most of *II./Fall.Rgt.9* remained in Honsfeld and only some elements continued to follow the Tiger II. At the same time that Peiper's men were breaking into Honsfeld, Sternebeck's *Spitze* intercepted an American convoy and other enemy unis soon after, as the SS officer himself recounts:"…*At 6:00, our point units caught a truck column by surprise coming from Büllingen, to the north of Honsfeld. The column was stopped by a blinking red lantern. It was an eight-truck resupply column. It was taken without firing a shot. Continuing towards Büllingen, at approximately 7:00, we came under fire from automatic weapons between 1,500 and 2,000 met4ers south of the city and west of our direction of march. The lead tanks quickly responded to the fire and attacked an airfield where there were several reconnaissance aircraft. Peiper called us back and ordered us to quickly resume the advance to capture Büllingen*". Peiper wanted to capture Büllingen because he counted on finding an American fuel dump there where he could refuel his vehicles. While the advance elements continued towards Büllingen, the capture of the American airstrip south of the town was entrusted to the heavy weapons platoon of the *10(gep.)/SS-Pz.Gr.Rgt.2* under *SS-Ustuf.* Werner Aschendorff. When Preuss's men later reached the vicinity of Büllingen, they came under enemy fire emanating from the first houses in the village. Around a hundred meters from the entrance to the place, a PzKpfw IV was knocked out by a bazooka and all of its crew were killed by enemy automatic weapons fire while they tried to abandon the tank.

SS-Osftuf. Preuss then pushed into the village with two SPW, sowing great confusion among the enemy troops and making it easier for the *Kampfgruppe* to capture the position. *SS-Ostuf.* Werner Sternebeck recounted these encounters:"…*again on the road to Büllingen, at a point with little visibility a few hundred meters from the entrance of the village the* Panzer IV *in front of me was destroyed by infantry weapons. In a savage charge, with every weapon that could fire, the rest of the armored vehicles pushed into Büllingen. The enemy was in a state of total confusion; despite it all, we had still managed to take advantage of the element of surprise. The enemy was incapable of offering any type of resistance whatsoever*". To the west of Büllingen,

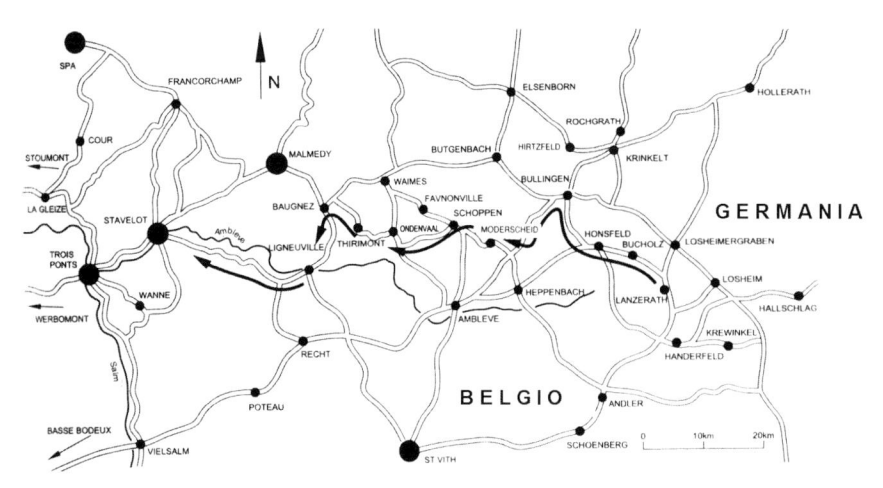

Moves of *Kampfgruppe Peiper*, from 4:00 to 23:00 on 17 December 1944.

LSSAH recon troops.

Peiper's men found the fuel dump, which was quickly emptied with the help of about fifty American prisoners. Along the road, equipment and supplies abandoned by the fleeing enemy were salvaged. *SS-Sturmmann* Helmut Neumann, of *12.Kp./2*, wrote in that regard that: "*...More than anything else I remember that at that moment of the advance we took possession of a huge quantity of material. American tanks had been abandoned by the edge of the road and we found cans of real coffee and also a great amount of chocolate*".

After having passed through Büllingen, Sternebeck's point elements got lost and instead of heading to the west, turned northwards towards Wirzfeld. On the edge of that village, it came under fire from several American tank destroyers; *SS-Oscha*. Wein's PzKpfw IV was knocked out and Sternebeck then turned back towards Büllingen in order to take the road to the woods at Bütgenbach. Moving towards Möderscheid, he thus got back on *Rollbahn D*, rejoining the *Kampfgruppe* and taking the lead again. At that moment, Sternebeck's leading element was left with only two PzKpfw IV tanks and two SPW.

After having refueled, the *Kampfgruppe* continued its march, towards Ligneuville; taking muddy roads, the *Panzergruppe* passed through Möderscheid, Schoppen and Ondenvaal without encountering any resistance by the enemy and several American vehicles that were unlucky enough to run into the German units were captured, among them four jeeps with two officers and nine men of the 32nd Armored Regiment's reconnaissance company. Shortly before reaching Thirimont, another enemy jeep was intercepted with an American lieutenant colonel aboard. *SS-Ostubaf*. Peiper got into the jeep and interrogated him, discovering that the headquarters of the U.S. 49th Antiaircraft Artillery Brigade was near Ligneuville and that the Americans were unaware of the exact position of his *Kampfgruppe*. The advance of the SS troops continued and around 11:00 Thirimont was reached. The *10.(gep.)/SS-Pz.Gr.Rgt.2* then moved on to the west, across the country roads and fields, attempting to reach the Malmedy-Ligneuville road (N23) and capture the American headquarters located there. Because of the terrible conditions of the ground, the *Panzergruppe* was prevented from taking this shortcut, having to take a longer

A Tiger of *s.SS-Pz.Abt.501* and two motorcyclists of *SS-Kampfgruppe Peiper* overtaking a column of American prisoners. (U.S.Army)

A German soldier inspects a half-track abandoned by the enemy.

American prisoners captured by the Germans in the Ardennes. (NA)

German Panthers on the march in the forests of the Ardennes.

route. After the leading tanks had left Thirimont and continued their advance, the men discovered a column of American tanks about seven hundred meters to their left.

This column was first spotted by troops led by *SS-Ostuf.* Werner Sternebeck, about 800-1,200 meters from the Baugnez crossroads. The leading elements opened fire on the moving column when it was two to three hundred meters from the crossroads. According to Sternebeck: "*...A number of vehicles caught fire immediately and the column scattered. The men jumped off and took cover. This was the moment to push immediately forward towards the crossroads, by the Weismes-Baugnez road. Even before we reached the crossroads we were under fire from machine guns and carbines fired by the tank crews who had gotten out of their tanks. We immediately returned their fire with our on-board machine guns and quickly attacked the immobilized column. When my tank was sixty or seventy meters from the column, the Americans came out from under their cover, raised their hands and surrendered. Then we slowly approached the column. (..) I reported my encounter with the enemy, the firefight and the results to the* Panzergruppe *via radio. Once again I gave the order to continue on towards Ligneuville without wasting any time*".

The Malmedy Massacre

The American column that had been intercepted by Sternebeck was in reality Battery B of the 285th Field Artillery Observation Battalion. The battle did not last long and resulted in the capture of 150 American soldiers, who were assembled in a field, while the *Kampfgruppe* continued its march towards Ligneuville. A bit later, around 14:00, shots were heard, followed by bursts of machine gun fire; dozens of prisoners had been killed by the SS troops. Some of them managed to save themselves and reach friendly lines. In all, eighty-six American soldiers were executed near the Baugnez crossroads, in what has become known in history as the "Malmedy massacre". According to some German accounts, the attempted escape by some American prisoners triggered the firing and gave rise to the tragedy. Near the crossroads, where the massacre took place, the *ii.Kp./12* passed by but did not stop, because it had been ordered to continue on towards Ligneuville. *SS-Stubaf.* Poetschke's Panther had stopped because of mechanical problems. At least five SPW of *9.(Pi.) Kp./SS-Pz.Rgt.1* under *SS-Ostuf.* Rumpf, passed along route N32. Another engineer platoon, from *3.(gep)Lp./ SS-Pz.Pi.-Btl.1*, led by *SS-Oscha.* Max Beutner, was assigned to watch the prisoners.

The atmosphere in the SS troops was not the happiest; Poetschke was in a foul mood because of his battalion's delay in the march schedule, because of his broken-down tank and by the refusal by the captured American drivers to drive their vehicles to the rear. At that moment, the PzKpfw IV of the 3rd Platoon of *7.Kp./SS-Pz.Rgt.1* arrived, moving along the N32 road, coming from the east. Two PzKpfw IV crossed a field to reach the N32. It was then that Poetschke ordered his engineers to open fire on the prisoners. *SS-Ostuf.* Rumpf and *SS-Ustuf.* Günter Hering advanced with their men towards the Americans. The order to open fire also involved Max Beutner and the crews of his SPW. *SS-Oscha.* Hans Siptrott also showed up with his PzKpfw IV near the Baugnez crossroads. Stopped by Beutner, he was ordered to shoot against the prisoners with his main gun, but he refused to do so, feigning to have no more ammunition. What might have appeared to be an incident became a war crime at the moment that the SS soldiers walked amongst the bodies of the Americans on the ground to "finish off" the wounded[13].

---
[13] According to the autopsies carried out by the Americans, forty men had been killed by a bullet in the head at close range.

Aerial view of the Baugnez crossroads, where the massacre occurred.

A column of American prisoners escorted by the Germans. (IWM)

An SS Panther in the Ardennes forest.

SS-Hstuf. Werner Poetschke.

SS-Rttf. Hans Siptrott.

German grenadiers in the Ardennes.

After having passed through the Baugnez crossroads, Sternebeck's lead elements reached Ligneuville around 13:45, taking control of the bridge that was located there. The headquarters of the 49th AAA Brigade had managed to escape just a few minutes earlier. *SS-Ustuf.* Arndt Fischer, adjutant of *SS-Pz.Rgt.1*, arrived with his Panther shortly afterwards[14]: "…*Behind me was the SPW with Peiper and Diefenthal. I drove through the village with the utmost caution and after having noted that there had been no clashes, I speeded up towards the bridge. Near the curve before the bridge, I was hit in the rear. Hidden behind a house, a tank had caught me in a trap. Sternebeck had had the advantage of having arrived first, exploiting the element of surprise. When we abandoned our vehicle, we were fired upon from nearby houses. We were burning like human torches, because only a few hours earlier we had supplied out tanks with gas cans and our uniforms were still soaked with gasoline. Peiper, who wanted to provide me with covering fire from his SPW, was able to keep the enemy soldiers away from us. Except for our driver our comrade Wolfgang Simon, all of the crew was able to get out of the vehicle… The units that arrived later cleared out the area. The enemy tank was*

---

[14] P. Agte, *Jochem Peiper. Commander Panzerregiment Leibstandarte*, page 484.

destroyed". To the east of Ligneuville, the *10.Kp./2* clashed with elements of the U.S. 14th Armored Battalion. When the units had regrouped in Ligneuville itself, Peiper discussed continuing the attack towards Stavelot with his unit commanders and then with the division commander himself, *SS-Oberführer* Mohnke. Around 17:00 on that same day of 17 December 1944, *Panzergruppe Peiper* moved towards the west, crossing particularly bad terrain, passing through Pont Beaumont and Lodomez, along the road to Stavelot, before reaching the bridge over the Amblève River.

The attack against Stavelot

Peiper's men continued to march in the total darkness of the night. They pushed on ahead until they had reached the suburbs of Stavelot, around midnight on 17 December. The SS armored grenadiers made an initial assault against the city, but were rebuffed by heavy fire from American batteries. Peiper therefore decided to postpone any other attacks until the following day. Let us read the text of a letter by Peiper, written in 1967, when he reached Stavelot[15]: "...*We tried to enter the city, but Stavelot is a small natural fortress, and an enormous rock protects its access. As soon as the first of our tanks, a Panzer IV, got past that obstacle and had made the curve that the road makes at that point, it was knocked out. The configuration of the terrain did not allow my tanks to get off the road and fan out. While the column waited on the road (all of the men were sleeping) small infantry squads deployed to cover the flanks. Soon after, we were subjected to a counterattack on the left flak by an American unit of more or less platoon strength*".

During the night between 17 and 18 December, Peiper set up his forward command post in a house in the western part of the village of Vaulx-Richard; for the attack against Stavelot, Peiper designated the *1.SS-Pz.Rgt.1* under *SS-Ostuf.* Kremser and the *2./SS-Pz.Rgt.1* under *SS-Ostuf.* Christ, both equipped with Panther tanks, while the mission of capturing the bridge at Stavelot was assigned to *11.(gep.)/SS-Pz.Gr.Rgt.2* led by *SS-Ostuf.* Heinz Tomhardt, who had only two platoons available, reinforced by some engineers from the *9./SS-Pz.Rgt.1*.

The other two companies of *SS-Pz.Rgt.1*, the *6.Kp.* and the *7.Kp.*, both equipped with PzKpfw IV tanks, were instead to advance to the south of the Amblève, with the mission of securing the crossing over the river at Trois-Ponts.

Around 02:00. *SS-Ostuf.* Tomhardt made his men of the 1st and 4th platoons, led by *SS-Ustuf.* Willi Horn and *SS-Oscha.* Rudi Rayer, dismount from their SPW. After having reached Stokeu, a suburb of the city, on foot, they were able to seize control of the bridge with a rapid assault. Or at least, so it seemed, because

December 1944: the bridge over the Amblève River at Stavelot.

Panther tanks during an attack in a village. (NA)

SS soldiers during the Ardennes offensive, December 1944.

---
[15] J. Lucas. *L'ultimo anno dell'esercito tedesco*. Hobby & Work italiana editrice, page 187

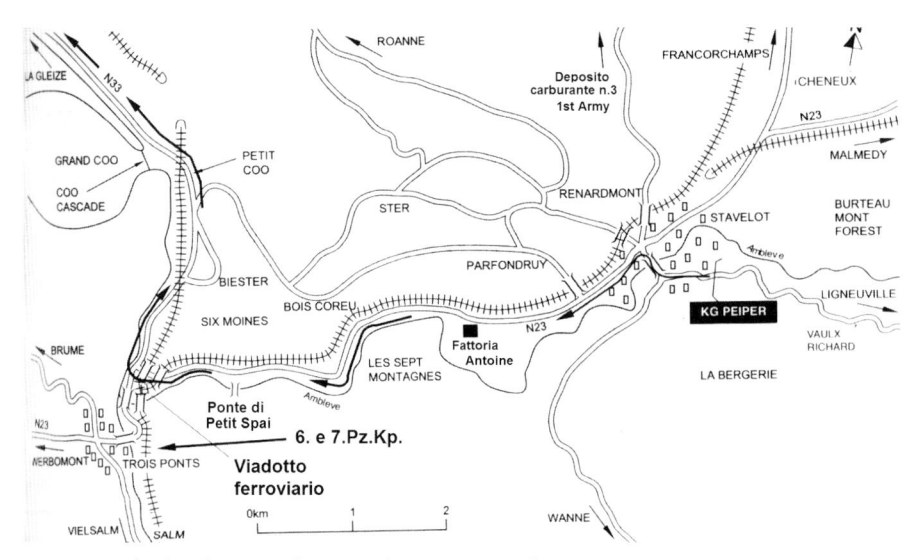

Movement of units of *SS-Kampfgruppe* Peiper on 18 December 1944.

SS-Hstuf. Josef Diefenthal.

they shortly came under heavy enemy fire; *SS-Ostuf.* Tomhardt was wounded, while *SS-Ustuf*, Horn and some other men were killed. By order of *SS-H*stuf. Diefenthal, *SS-Oscha.* Rudolf Rayer assumed command of the company. Under those conditions, however, the SS grenadiers could not continue to defend the bridge, because, meanwhile, American tanks had appeared on the opposite bank of the river. While the grenadiers of *11.Kompanie* were "hanging on" to the houses south of the river, the attack by the panzers against Stavelot was launched at 8:00.

The plan, drawn up by Peiper, repeated the tactics that had already been employed on the Eastern Front: first it was necessary to secure the area south of the bridge, then a company of Panthers would be sent forward over the bridge, to break into the city, leaving the infantry units to mop up the city. And thus, after a brief covering fire by artillery and mortars, the tanks descended down the long road that led into the valley, with *SS-Oscha.* Erich Strelow's Panther in the lead. From a report written by Werner Poetschke: "*...when I reached the city, Strelow was pointing to a curve, when suddenly I saw two anti-tank guns fifty meters away protecting the important bridge, at the entrance to the town.* SS-Oberscharführer *Strelow immediately realized that the bridge was of great importance to the battalion's advance and had to be taken. The enemy opened fire furiously against the tank with the anti-tank guns and infantry weapons. Without hesitating for a moment, Strelow moved towards the two anti-tank guns, overran the first and then headed towards the second, reserving the same fate for it, took the bridge, and thus opened the way into the city.*". The attack, however, cost *SS-Ostuf.* Kremser dearly, as he was badly wounded during the fighting. His Panther "111" was hit by enemy fire, right on the middle of the bridge. *SS-Ustuf.* Hans Hennecke then took

A Panther tank hit at Stavelot, 18 December 1944.

The bridge at Stavelot, damaged by the fighting.

command of *1.Pz.Kp.*. The lead Panther, although hit by American anti-tank guns, was able to break through the weak barrier erected by the defenders. The second Panther went at full speed over the stone bridge as did the other Panthers which followed it, taking the southern part of the city. The Americans reacted by counterattacking on the left of the *Kampfgruppe*: the men of *III. (gep.)/SS-Pz.Gr.Rgt.2* under Diefenthal warded them off and advanced towards the bridge to ensure its control. The defenders then attempted to resist in the center of the city, shifting their armored units towards the bridge and on the hills that overlooked the German positions.

A Panther tank in the streets of Stavelot.

A German soldier killed in the fighting on the square at Stavelot.

The bridges over the Amblève at Trois-Ponts.

An American anti-tank gun in firing position. (NA)

Once inside Stavelot, the SS units were met by violent enemy fire; a tough and bitter battle between armored vehicles followed, which lasted about two hours. While the fighting was still raging, around 10:00 the leading elements of the *Kampfgruppe* succeded in advancing as far as the market square, then turning to the west and exiting the city, taking road N23 towards Trois-Ponts.

SS-Ostubaf. Peiper did not think it suitable to stop to secure total control of Stavelot, because the priority was to reach the Meuse in the shortest time possible. *"…When we broke into Stavelot, many civilians fired on us from the windows of their houses. At that moment, my only objective was to reach the bridge near Trois-Ponts. In any case, there was no time to lose with these civilians and we had to continue our march, even though I knew that resistance in this city had not been completely eliminated"*.

Trois-Ponts

The men of the *Panzergruppe* then continued along the northern bank of the Amblève and soon reached Trois-Ponts, a city that was located at the confluence of the rivers Amblève and Salm. The three bridges over the river, two railway and one road, had been mined by the Americans. Peiper decided to attack the position with a pincer movement: the bulk of his *Kampfgruppe* was to advance along the northern bank on *Rollbahn D*, while the 6. and the *7.Kp./SS-Pz.Gr.Rgt.1*, supported by *3.(gep.)Kp./SS-Pz.Pi.-Btl.1*, were to reach Trois-Ponts, passing through Henumont and Wanne. Just before Trois-Ponts, a double railway viaduct stood over the road to Stavelot. An American 75mm anti-tank gun was in position precisely at that point and stopped the first Panther. The second, commanded by *SS-Oscha*. Strelow, was able to neutralize it. Soon after, the *Kampfgruppe* began to attack the position at Trois-Ponts. But, at 11:15, the bridge over the Amblève was blown into the air, crashing into the river. Meanwhile, the group coming from Wanne made it up the hill, but at 13:00, when the leading SS vehicles approached the bridge over the Salm River, that bridge also was blown

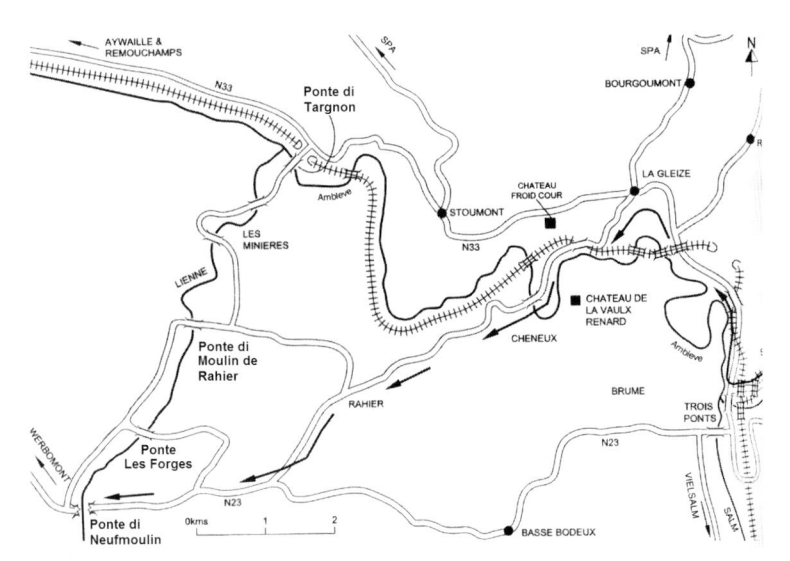

Movement of SS units from Trois-Ponts to Neufmoulin.

A formation of P-47 thunderbolts in flight.

A Panther knocked out by American anti-tank guns at Neufmoulin.

into the air, in front of the eyes of the SS soldiers. The *6.Kp./SS-Pz.Rgt.1* and the *3.(gep).Kp./SS-Pz. Pi.-Btl.1*, then returned to Stavelot, while the *7.Kp./ SS-Pz.Rgt.1* remained under cover in Wanne, for lack of fuel. Initially, it seemed that Peiper intended to turn to the south, but the destruction of the bridges forced him to continue the advance to the north, remaining on the N33 road. His advance guard, now consisting only of the *1.Kp./SS-Pz.Rgt.1* under *SS-Ustuf.* Hans Hennecke, passed through Coo and reached the village of La Gleize at 13:00. Half an hour later, near Cheneux, a bridge was captured intact over the Amblève River; there was now the possibility of being able to continue to the southwest, to return to the N23, which led from Trois-Ponts to Werbomont. This would have turned the *Panzergruppe* around, towards the designated attack route. But just at that moment, for the first time since the beginning of the offensive, the skies cleared and the heavy cloud cover that had protected Peiper's march from Allied aviation disappeared almost completely; soon after, at 13:25, four P-47 Thunderbolts attacked the *Panzergruppe* columns, followed at 14:40 by another twenty Thunderbolts that hit the entire march column between the positions of Lodomez and Stavelot.

But even more serious was the fact that the Americans had now identified the direction of march of Peiper's *Kampfgruppe* and could thus prepare to destroy the bridges along the route. And that is what happened. After having lost three tanks, five SPW and other vehicles to air attacks, the *Panzergruppe* resumed its march around 16:30, when it became dark; there were still two bridges to cross before reaching the Meuse. The first was over the Lienne River, at Neufmoulin, the second over the River Ourthe, near Hamoir. Peiper sent his advance force to capture the bridge over the Lienne, but as soon as the first tanks approached it, the Americans blew the bridge at Neufmoulin. Patrols from *III.(gep.)/2* were also sent to the north of Neufmoulin, where there were another two bridges over the Lienne. The *11.Kp./2* was able to capture the one at Chauveheid intact, while the *10.Kp./2* captured the bridge at Rahier. Unfortunately, neither of the two bridges was solid enough to support the weight of the panzers. The *11.Kp./2* then returned to the south, reaching the demolished bridge at Neufmoulin; in the darkness, the SS grenadiers were not able to find the N23 again and after having wandered off towards Troude-Bras, they were called back. The men of *10.Kp./2* also lost their way. After having crossed through Chevron and Habiemont, outside of Oufni they were checked by several enemy tanks; in the fighting that followed, the company lost four of its SPW and fifteen grenadiers. Not having available any material and equipment to construct a passage for his panzers, Peiper decided to bring his *Kampfgruppe* back to La Gleize, leaving *Flak.Abt.84* to protect the bridge over the Amblève at Cheneux. Around 23:00, the bulk of Peiper's column halted in a wooded area, between Stoumont and La Gleize,

18 December 1944, at the Kaiserbaracke crossroads on *Rollbahn E*: Kurt Sowa's Tiger "222", of s.SS-Pz.Abt.501 with four paratroopers of FJR 9 on board. The march route was along N23, between Saint-Vith and Malmédy. (US Army).

SS-Stubaf. Knittel, on the right, with SS-Ostuf. Leidriter. (US Army).

where it was joined by part of the elements that had been left at Wanne[16] and by *s.SS-Pz.Abt.501*, mainly the *2.Kp.* under *SS-Hstuf.* Rolf Möbius and a platoon of the *3.Kp.* under *SS-Hstuf.* Heinz Birnschein. Some Tiger II tanks of *1.Kp./s.SS-Pz.Abt.501* had managed to cross the Amblève at Stavelot, but only one of them was able to join up with the *Kampfgruppe*, while the others were broken down with mechanical problems.

A little later, the *5.Bttr./SS-Pz.Art.Rgt.1* under *SS-Ostuf.* Butschek and elements of *SS-Pz.Aufkl.-Abt.1* reached La Gleize. At about 24:00, Pieper decided to change his *Kampgruppe's* direction of march, proceeding to the west, across the valley of the Amblève. During the night, Peiper learned that Stavelot had not yet been cleared of enemy forces and this prevented the arrival of supplies for his *Kampfgruppe*. And so, *I./SS-Pz.art.-Rgt.1* and most of *s.SS-Pz.Abt.501* had not been able to make their way across the city; there were twenty-two PzKpfw IV, nine Panthers and twenty-seven Tiger II stalled to the south of Stavelot,

either because of mechanical problems or for lack of fuel. Peiper had been left with six Tigers, nineteen Panthers and six PzKpfw IV and a good number of SPW. *SS-Ostubaf.* Peiper then ordered *SS-Stubaf.* Knittel, commander of *SS-Pz.Aufkl.-Abt.1*, to return to Stavelot in the morning, to open the road from the west, while along with *SS-Stubaf.* Poetschke and *SS-Hstuf.* Diefenthal, he planned the attack against the position at Stoumont. At the same time, *SS-Gruf.* Priess, commander of *I.SS-Pz.Korps*, ordered *SS-Obf.* Mohnke to have all of the other units of the *Leibstandarte* to converge behind Peiper's *Kampfgruppe*, to resume the advance to the Meuse. The movements of the German units around the Stoumont area pushed the Americans, during that same night, to significantly reinforce the position, bringing in many tanks and anti-tank guns.

The attack against Stoumont

During the early hours of 19 December 1944, the Panthers of *2.Kp./SS-Pz.Rgt.1* of *SS-Ostuf.* Friedrich Christ and several PzKpfw IV of *6.Kp./SS-Pz.Rgt.1* moved from their positions at Froide-Cour, moving along road N33 towards Stoumont, clashing with the first enemy units around 7:00. At the same time, *9.(gep.)/SS-Pz.Gr.Rgt.2* under *SS-Ustuf.* Max Leike and the *9.(Pi.)/SS-Pz.Rgt.1* led by *SS-Ostuf.* Erich Rumpf, along with a group of paratroopers, moved through the woods to attack Stoumont from the south. Tanks and Panzergrenadiers launched their attack, but were not able to deploy over a wide front because of the lay of the ground: there was a ravine on the left side of the road. The SS troops were able to neutralize an enemy anti-tank position before it was able to open fire. The Panthers approached Stoumont from the east, but came under violent fire from American anti-tank guns and armored vehicles that were positioned on the edge of the village. A group of five Sherman tanks of the 743rd Tank Battalion, after having engaged in a quick exchange of fire with the German tanks, pulled back to the church at Stoumont. This missed victory threw *SS-Stubaf.* Poetschke into a rage, who railed against his tankers, ordering them to attack again immediately. Hans-Georg Hüber, the gunner in the lead tank, relates[17]: "…*We had taken numerous anti-tank rounds coming from the direc-*

---

[16] Proposal for the citation in the *Wehrmacht* Bulletin of Honor for Erich Strelow, dated 28 December 1944.

[17] Because of the lack of fuel, only five panzers of *6.Kp./SS-Pz.Rgt.1* and only one of *7.Kp.*, as also most of *3.(gep.)Kp./SS-Pz.Pi.-Btl.1* reached Peiper at La Gleize. The rest of the units were stalled at Wanne, under *SS-Ostuf.* Sternebeck.

SS-Ostuf. Friedrich Christ. (BDC)

A Panther in the streets of Stoumont. In the foreground are destroyed American vehicles.

An SS Panther during the attack on Stoumont.

Panthers of *Kampfgruppe Peiper* on the outskirts of Stoumont; the tank in the lead is in flames after having taken a direct hit.

tion of the church. Our turret was frozen. Despite that, I tried to spot the enemy anti-tank gun, but at that moment were hit again, this time in the engine compartment. At that point the tank began to burn…". A 90mm gun was in fact set up to the east of the church of Stoumont. Three Panthers then attacked on the left of the main road in order to engage the enemy anti-tank guns. Two SPW, one armed with a 75mm gun and the other with a *Drillingsflak* (a twin anti-aircraft gun) were destroyed.

Let us follow the course of the battle, reading the text of the citation for the award of the Oak Leaves to *SS-Stubaf.* Werner Poetscheke, written by Peiper himself[18]: *"…The attack, made immediately, soon reached a dead spot, because the road was effectively blocked by fire from anti-tank and anti-aircraft guns in the suburbs of the village, as also by fire from enemy tanks in the woods on the northern edge of Stoumont. In clear recognition of the fact that only a bold advance could be successful, even at the cost of his life, Poetschke put himself at the head of his tanks and threw himself into the attack to act as an example. Despite that, the attack was not successful and several vehicles began to slowly back away in order to take cover behind a slope. At that critical moment, Poetschke was seized by a strong sense of rage. He climbed down from his tank, grabbed a* Panzerfaust *and threatened to fire on his own crew if they took one more step backward. This brutal measure was decisive to raise the morale of the men. Paying no heed to the deadly fire and to his own losses, the tanks broke into the city, firing savagely, spreading havoc among the enemy lines, breaking their dogged resistance. One hundred fifty prisoners, four anti-aircraft guns, five heavy anti-tank guns, four Shermans and a great quantity of equipment fell into our hands"*.

The fighting for Stoumont lasted about two hours, until the American tanks began to withdraw

---

[18] P. Agte. *Jochen Peiper. Commander Panzerregiment Leibstandarte*, page 488.

to the west, abandoning their infantry. Peiper then ordered *SS-Hstuf.* Diefenthal to pursue the enemy. The *11.Kp./2* thus moved forward, with *SS-Oscha.* Walter Ropeter's Panther in the lead. When they got close to the Stoumont station about three kilometers to the northwest, the SS troops were met by units of the U.S. 119th Infantry Regiment supported by tanks: twelve Shermans, four tank destroyers and a company of infantry supported by two artillery batteries. The Sherman tanks quickly opened fire, hitting the first SS Panthers; Ropeter's Panther "225" was hit and began to burn. Panthers "212" and "233" met the same fate, while *SS-Ustuf.* Hubert Kaufmann's Panther "211" managed to pull back in time. *SS-Oscha.* Rayer's *11.Kp./2* also suffered heavy losses, due mainly to enemy artillery fire. When it began to get dark, the fighting resumed in the sector to the west of Stoumont station. There were not enough German troops to defend the three kilometers that separated Stoumont from its station; the Americans attacked on both sides of the road to Stoumont with tank support. And so, around 21:00, after Peiper had consulted with Poetschke, he ordered all of his units to fall back on Stoumont and with that final action, the advance of the *Kampfgruppe* to the Meuse could be considered to have been essentially at an end. Without fuel and low on ammunition, Peiper was forced to assume a defensive posture to at least hold on to the positions that had been taken up to that time. His men were now bottled up in a tight area between La Gleize, Stoumont and Cheneux.

Holding the positions

After having moved his command post to the castle at Froide-Cour, halfway between La Gleize and Stoumont along the N23 road, Peiper issued new orders to the units: the *2.Kp./SS-Pz.Rgt.1* was to hold the position at Stoumont with the support of *3.(gep.)Kp/SS-Pz.Pi.-Btil.1*, while a platoon of *Flakpanzer IV* and the paratroop units, while the defense of La Gleize was assigned to the PzKpfw IV, the *1.Kp./SS-Pz.Rgt.1* and the *9.(Pi.)Kp./SS-Pz.Rgt.1*. Six Tiger II tanks were assigned to defend the roads from the north and northeast. The *III.(gep.)/2* split its men between Stoumont and Cheneux. *Flak-Abt.84* still defended the bridge over the Amblève at Cheneaux. Throughout the entire night of 20 December, American artillery incessantly shelled the Stoumont and Cheneux

SS Panther tanks and grenadiers entering Stoumont, engaging in tough fighting in the streets. (US Army)

***SS-Stubaf.* Poetschke with a *Panzerfaust*, to use against approaching enemy tanks.**

Fallschirmjäger following *Kampfgruppe Peiper*, fighting at Stoumont. (US Army).

An American prisoner captured in Stoumont.

A Panther and a *Flakpanzer IV* crossing through Stoumont, moving to the west, towards the station.

sectors, creating great confusion in the German lines and causing new losses; while he was withdrawing with the remnants of his company at Cheneaux, *SS-Oscha*. Rayer was wounded as a result of the enemy shelling. He was then brought to the cellars of the castle of Stoumont, where a first aid station had been set up and where some wounded American prisoners were being treated.

At first light on the day of 20 December, the Americans attacked the *Kampfgruppe Peiper* positions in force, from all sides, from Stoumont as far as La Gleize. A massive attack by American tanks against Stoumont was fended off; on the eastern edge of the village, the fighting developed into bitter house-to-house combat. Also to the north of Stoumont, attacks by American troops were rebuffed after furious encounters. Peiper was forced to throw all of his reserves into the battle. At Cheneux, the artillerymen of *Flak-Bataillon 84* and the grenadiers of *11.(gep.)/SS-Pz.Rgt.2* tenaciously defended their positions after a pitched battle against troops of the U.S. 82nd Airborne Division. The *II./SS-Pz.Gr.Rgt.2* under *SS-Hstuf*. Herbert Schnelle, after having managed to penetrate the village from the east, reaching La Gleize, quickly sent his *6.Kp.*, under *SS-Ostuf*. Schenk, to support the defenders of Cheneaux.

Around noontime, an American armored formation consisting of about forty tanks began to move from La Gleize, moving in the direction of the Roane-Trois Ponts road. Without fuel and with only limited ammunition available, *SS-Ostubaf*. Peiper was unable to carry out any counterattack, finding himself with his *Panzergruppe* completely surrounded by American forces. The American forces continued to attack in the Cheneux and Stoumont sectors, stopped only by the stubborn resistance of the SS grenadiers of the SPW battalion.

The sanctuary of St. Edward, on the northwest edge of the village, became a critical point for the defense of Stoumont. Defending it were the *3.(gep.)/SS-Pz.Pi.Btl.1* under *SS-Ostuf*. Franz Sievers, elements of *9.(Pi.)/SS-Pz.Rgt.1* and some paratroopers. Sievers was ordered to defend the northeastern and southern edges of Stoumont, receiving five tanks as reinforcement. Several days later, Peiper described Sievers' action at Stoumont[19] as follows: "...*Against overwhelming American infantry, which attacked tenaciously with the support of tanks, Sievers, along with three other men, was pushed back into a room of the sanatorium. With*

---

[19] *Personalakte Werner Poetschke*, Berlin Document Center.

Aerial view of Stoumont, with the principal places of *Kampfgruppe Peiper's* encounters.

SS-Ustuf. Franz Sievers. (BDC)

Stoumont, December 1944: *SS-Ostubaf.* Peiper, second from the left, discussing the situation with his soldiers in the presence of several American prisoners.

Panzerfausts and hand grenades, he fought from room to room, knocking down all the Americans he ran across and with his pistol was able to keep the infantry confined to the cellar. After a tank had blown away the second floor with a main gun round, he was the first to push into the cellar and to wipe out the enemy after a furious fight. The Americans repeated their attacks several times and each time thought that they could enter the sanatorium because of their numerical superiority. Thanks to the fanatical will of SS-Ostuf. Sievers, coupled with his exceptional command ability and his superhuman courage, the sanatorium remained firmly in our hands. This also guaranteed freedom of movement for the entire Panzergruppe, which was already compressed into a very limited area".

The sanatorium of St. Edward was finally captured by American troops during the night. A counterattack by SS troops resulted in the capture of about forty prisoners and destruction of three American tanks.

The loss of Cheneux

In the early hours of 21 December the fighting shifted to Cheneaux, attacked by units of the 82nd Airborne Division. Earlier during the night the American paratroopers had attacked but were driven back.

At 8:00, after half an hour of preparatory artillery fire, the Germans counterattacked to try to recapture the western part of the village, but were in turn driven off, suffering heavy losses. Throughout the day, other American forces advanced and captured Monceau, a small village south of Cheneux. As enemy pressure intensified, at 17:00 the forces defending Cheneux were ordered to withdraw to La Gleize. The Americans continued to attack Cheneux, finally taking it. Let us read the brief summary of the attack written by the commander of the 82nd Airborne Division, General James Maurice Gavin:

"...The fighting at Cheneaux intensified. On that date [21 December], the First Battalion of the 504th, supported by a company of that regiment's Third Battalion, made a final assault against the German positions in this city; after hand-to-hand fighting, during which our paratroopers jumped aboard the German half-tracks and engaged the German soldiers with knives, the remaining enemy forces were thrown back across the Amblève River and our troops took control of the bridge. During this attack, we destroyed a considerable number of tanks and killed or captured many soldiers of the 1.SS-Panzer-Division".

When the final assault against Cheneux was made, the SS troops had already pulled back towards La Gleize, leaving only a small rearguard. Because of the lack of fuel, Peiper's men had to leave behind fourteen *Flak* guns, five 105mm howitzers, two *Pak 40*, six SPW and five trucks. Furious fighting also erupted near the Werimont farm, along the road that ran from La Gleize to Trois Ponts, which mainly involved the tank of *SS-Hstuf.* Oskar Klingelhöfer, the Tiger II of *SS-Ustuf.* Georg Hantusch and of *SS-Ostuf.* Wilhelm Dollinger and several Panthers.

Withdrawal to La Gleize

Once all hope of continuing the advance had vanished and knowing that he could not defend Cheneux and Stoumont with the few available forces, *SS-Ostubaf.* Peiper decided to have his *Kampfgruppe* pull back to La Gleize, maintaining control over the bridge at Cheneux. Around 14:00, and American combat group of the 119th Inf.Rgt., consisting mainly of engineers, was able to cut the road between Stoumont and La Gleize, felling the trees that lined it, after which they mined the road as well. The *10.Kp./2* counterattacked, managing to push back the American engineers and to capture the enemy commander, Major McCown. The abandonment of Stoumont was carried out in the early evening without any interference from the Americans. Following that withdrawal, the castle at Froide-Cour fell outside of the defensive perimeter. The wounded who could walk and about a hundred American prisoners were moved to La Gleize. The badly wounded were left in the care of a German surgeon and two American medical orderlies.

The village of La Gleize consisted of about thirty houses and bitter fighting ensued for the possession of each of them. In the afternoon of the 22nd, the Americans made a series of attacks along all of the roads that led to La Gleize; many close-range clashes ensued, but in the end, the attackers were rebuffed and the SS troops were able to eliminate all of the American penetrations. The American artillery then joined the action, unleashing a hurricane of fire on La Gleize; phosphorous shells set all of the houses on fire and an artificial fog began to envelop the entire sector. Let us read the account by *SS-Ustuf.* Rolf Reiser, Werner Poetschke's adjutant[20]: "...*After several hours, the enemy had not attacked and we had by now become accustomed to the never-ending artillery fire. The shelling*

[20] *Personalakte Franz Sievers,.* Sievers would be cited in the Wehrmacht Bulletin of Honor following this action.

Panther "131" hit and abandoned, near the bridge at Cheneux, clearly visible in the background, on the left. (US Army)

Königstiger "222" with several *Fallschirmjäger* loaded on board.

Closeup of the turret of a King Tiger in the Ardennes. (DW).

began to slack off slowly during the course of the morning. In the defensive positions, contact with the unit commanders was possible only by courier. The couriers accomplished prodigious feats throughout the day, under deadly artillery fire and in full view of the enemy. At 14:00, the American artillery ceased its firing and an attack by infantry and tanks was made along each road that led into the village. SS-Ostubaf. Peiper gave the order: "...everyone out for the defense!". We had left the command post. Tank crews,

Stoumont, on the left, grenadiers and SS half-tracks engaged in combat, on the right, captured American prisoners.

Panorama of La Gleize, from a period post card.

Grenadiers of SS-*Kampgruppe Peiper*, armed with a *Panzerfaust*.

couriers and radio operators, armed with rifles, machine pistols and Panzerfaust, took up positions in the destroyed houses and awaited the enemy. A sharpshooter knelt down next to me, behind the destroyed wall of a house, beginning to take aim at American infantrymen who were advancing along the ditch next to the road. Counting on their numerical superiority, especially with respect to tanks, the Americans were able to reach the first houses on the roads leading to Stoumont and Borgoumont. Counterattacking and fighting ferociously house to house for several hours, we once again managed to drive off all of their attacks. The enemy ended his offensive action at dusk and withdrew…".

Fighting was also fierce near the farm at Werimont, as recounted by SS-*Rottenführer* Rolf Erhardt, driver of Oskar Klingelhöfer's tank[21]: "…*Many Shermans approached us along the road situated on the other side of a gully. The guns of our PzKpfw.IV were ineffective at that range. The Shermans were easy prey for the 88mm guns of our King Tigers and for the 75mm guns of the Panther which were superior at this range. The American unit was spotted early on and we let them come closer to a range that was favorable to us. After one of our Tigers had missed its first shot, to our great surprise the Shermans quickly opened fire. This forced me to hide in a house where I had an observation post on the second floor. From there, I could follow the course of the battle. The American shells continued to fall all around the house. The cellar was full of soldiers who were waiting for a lull in the fighting to count the number of Shermans that had been knocked out. The firing of our Tigers could be clearly distinguished from the explosions of the enemy shells. Within ourselves, we knew that every round fired by an 88 was a bullseye. All of a sudden, the tank commander, Hantusch, entered the cellar with his hands pressed to his head, shouting "…it's Hantusch's last stand.!". His Tiger had been hit several times and the electrical firing system had been damaged. Then a final round had hit the turret, wounding Hantusch in the head. He was forced to abandon the tank which was on fire. A few minutes later, the second tank commander, SS-Ostuf. Dollinger, came into the cellar quietly, bleeding profusely from his head. After having been treated, he reported that the smoke coming from his main gun made it impossible to see and fire. The numerical superiority of*

---

[21] Ralf Tiemann. *Die Leibstandarte. Vol IV/2*, pagees 134-135.

Hantusch's Tiger, knocked out near the Werimont farm.

A young German grenadier during the fighting.

SS grenadiers during a lull in the fighting.

An American Sherman in the Ardennes, December 1944.

the Shermans and their rapid fire had offset the superiority of the guns of our panzers. Dollinger's Tiger had also been hit by a round that had cut off the first third of his gun's barrel. A sense of depression began to snake its way through the air and in that ravine, forgotten by God, it seemed that everything was now against us…". Around 20:00, about twenty German aircraft dropped containers in the Stoumont area, thinking that the position was still in the hands of Peiper's men.

Only ten percent of those containers, containing fuel, were collected by the SS troops. That small bit of fuel was just enough to be able to start the engines of the vehicles in order to turn on the radios, while a few tanks managed to change positions. At the end of the day, the *I.SS-Pz. Korps* requested permission to withdraw *Kampfgruppe Peiper*, but the headquarters of *6.Panzerarmee* headquarters issued a categorical refusal. Peiper himself had requested to be allowed to withdraw from La Gleize in order to reach the *Leibstandarte* lines, finding himself completely unable to continue to defend the positions that had been reached, without ammunition and without fuel.

Breakout maneuver

On 23 December, American artillery intensified its shelling of Peiper's positions. A tank attack coming from Froide-Cour was stopped by a Panther and a PzKpfw IV near the Venne crossroads. That same day, the commander of the *I.SS-Pz.Korps*, *SS-Gruf.* Hermann Priess, aware that he could not help Peiper's men, ordered him to withdraw with his men and vehicles. Without even a drop of fuel, all of the vehicles and the wounded had to be left in place. In the afternoon of that same day, Peiper then decided to pass through the American lines, launching a desperate attack with his SS grenadiers, an attack that was to be unleashed soon after the *Kampfgruppe* had completed the destruction of all of its heavy weapons. *SS-Ostubaf.* Peiper consulted with his unit commanders and was also able to reach an agreement with the American officers who were prisoners, according to which once the group had withdrawn, the American officers would assume responsibility for the prisoners and all of the wounded. The medical officer of the *III./2* volunteered to remain to treat the wounded.

On 24 December, the remnants of *Kampfgruppe Peiper* left La Gleize, with less than a thousand men, marching on foot. Only a handful of soldiers remained in the village, with the mission of masking

SS-Ostuf. Dollinger's King Tiger "213" destroyed at La Gleize.

American tanks and infantry breaking into La Gleize, December 1944.

the departure of their comrades and to sabotage all of the abandoned vehicles; thirty armored vehicles and about a hundred half-tracks were destroyed. Between forced demolitions and combat losses, Peiper's *Kampfgruppe* had lost a total of ninety-two tanks, twenty-three artillery pieces, six self-propelled guns, twenty-five *Nebelwerfer* launchers, ninety-five half-tracks, seventy-seven trucks and two thousand men. At 2:00, the column moved from La Gleize, with Peiper in the lead, with only a small advance guard in front of him. When it reached Grume, the column set off to the north, towards Coo, to reach the lines held by *SS-Kampfgruppe Hansen*. But the bridge at Coo had been destroyed and therefore Peiper decided to have his men hide in the woods for the whole day in order to avoid being spotted by Allied air reconnaissance. The column resumed its march after noontime, across the N23 road between Basse-Bodeux and Trois-Ponts. The column reached the Salm River at dawn on 25 December, coming under enemy fire when the men began to cross the river. *SS-Ostubaf.* von Westernhagen crossed the river with a wounded man on his shoulders, while Peiper was wounded in the hand during the crossing. Shortly after, the positions of *SS-Pz.Gr.Rgt.1* were reached and Peiper quickly reported to *SS-Obf.* Mohnke in the castle of Wanne. Of the three thousand men of the *Kampfgruppe* that had crossed the Amblève a few days earlier, only 770 returned to friendly lines. Most of the equipment had been lost. On 26 December 1944, *Kampfgruppe Peiper* was officially disbanded.

The Knight's Cross with Oak Leaves and Swords

Despite the failure of his mission, Peiper was recommended for the Knight's Cross with Oak Leaves

A German grenadier. (DW).

American soldiers inspect an abandoned King Tiger. (US Army).

and Swords. During the course of the offensive, the *Kampfgruppe* had destroyed 27 enemy tanks, 15 armored cars, 35 half-tracks, 14 aircraft, 50 heavy anti-tank guns, 12 anti-aircraft guns and 180 wheeled vehicles. Following is the text of the citation written by *SS-Oberführer* Wilhelm Mohnke:

"… SS-Obersturmführer *Peiper took part in the fighting of the* Leibstandarte, *from August of 1941. He has already been awarded the Oak Leaves for his Knight's Cross, as commander of the division's armored group, demonstrating great composure, daring and determination in his decisions, all good characteristics for a unit commander. In*

SS grenadiers and *Luftwaffe* infantrymen. (US Army)

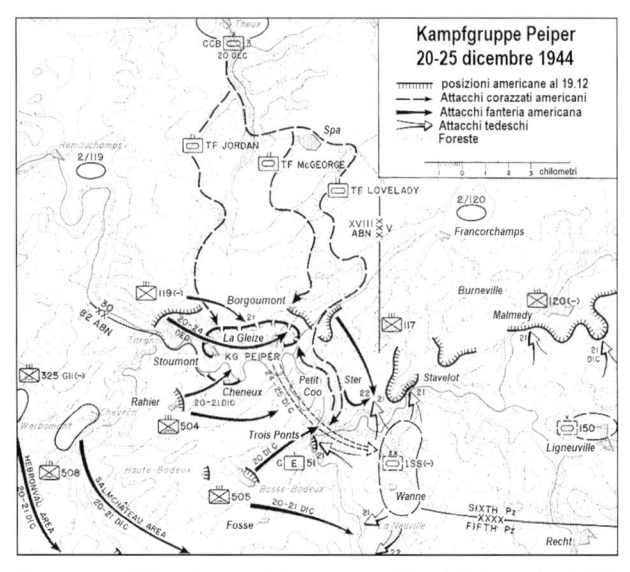

Kampfgruppe Hansen grenadiers.

Movements of *Kampfgruppe Peiper* between 20 and 25 December 1944.

all situations in which he found himself, he always showed himself to be a good commander. After having overcome the difficulties of the terrain and after having made contact with the 3.Fallschirmjäger-Division at Lanzerath, in the early morning hours of 17 December 1944 the armored group made a surprise push against Honsfeld, which was taken decisively, enabling the capture of a large American reconnaissance unit. After this success, he immediately continued the advance, reaching Büllingen. Despite strong enemy resistance, the attack carried out against the village allowed the capture of twelve enemy aircraft and numerous military items. Without worrying about his exposed flanks

and with only the thought of penetrating even deeper into the enemy lines, the armored group continued its march towards Engelsdorf, passing through Mödersheid-Schoppen-Faymonville and further on to Ligneuville. During the precipitous advance, near Baugnez, he destroyed an enemy supply column. Shortly after he found himself facing a blocking unit of the 49th Anti-Aircraft Brigade, which was also overrun and destroyed. Continuing to not worry about safeguarding his flanks, the group continued to advance, always with its commander in the lead. Wherever he went, the enemy fell and around evening he reached the outskirts of Stavelot. On the morning of 18 December 1944 he crossed the ground in front of Stavelot, favorable to the resistance of the new enemy positions, took possession of the bridge and continued immediately towards Trois-Ponts and towards La Gleize. By 14:30 the locality had been seized and after a bitter fight the men took up positions. The villages of Cheneux and Stoumont, despite stubborn enemy resistance, were also finally taken.

As a result of difficulties in obtaining fuel, the Kampfgruppe was forced to halt. The bulk of the other units, day after day, were forced to halt because, in front of the Armored Group, the enemy, despite heavy losses, was reinforcing. Beginning on 20 December 1944 and in the fourteen days that followed, the attacks against American armored divisions and infantry divisions became ineffective. When on 22 December 1944 SS-Ostubaf. Peiper came to the conclusion that the men in Stoumont and Cheneux might be

Peiper with the *Ritterkreuz mit Eichenlaub und Schwerten*.

surrounded, he made the decision to have them all withdraw to La Gleize. The advance of the units was by then interrupted and heroic fights for each meter of ground ensued. Despite the commander's will to fight and to advance, all of the attacks were rebuffed. On 23 December 1944, when no tanks were able to move and the last round had been fired, towards evening SS-Ostubaf. Peiper *received the order to withdraw. Bringing with it all of the remaining ammunition, the* Kampfgruppe *gathered eight hundred men and on 24 December, at 02:00, without being noticed by the enemy, reached the original main combat line, after marching for twenty-two hours, across hilly and heavily wooded terrain. Passing through the enemy lines, with great physical effort, the men reached Roglin Vale, where despite the fact that the enemy in that sector of the front was in a state of alert and searching for stragglers,* Kampfgruppe Peiper, *with a surprising but desperate advance, broke through enemy resistance and in large measure was able to reach the opposite bank of the river, where there were their own lines. It was during this event that Peiper, at the head of the* Kampfgruppe, *was wounded. Through the surprising coup by the group commanded by* SS-Ostubaf. Peiper, *which had made a deep penetration into the enemy sector, which marched with its men to the west, the enemy was forced to shift several divisions from the Aachen-Jülich area…".*

***SS-Ostubaf*. Jochen Peiper.**

The Hungarian Front

In January 1945, the Ardennnes offensive having failed and with the Soviet forces now on the borders of the *Reich*, Adolf Hitler made the decision to move Sepp Dietrich's *6.Panzerarmee* to the Hungarian front: the intention was to try to free Budapest, which was completely surrounded, arrest the enemy offensive aimed at the heart of the *Reich* and at the same time maintain control over the Hungarian oil fields, vital to the continuation of the German war effort. On 16 January, Dietrich was ordered to regroup and reorganize his units by the end of the month; at that time, his *6.Panzerarmee* consisted of the *I.SS-Pz.Korps* under *SS-Gruf.* Hermann Priess and the *II.SS-Pz.Korps* under *SS-Gruf.* Willi Bittrich. The new offensive on the Hungarian front was to be kept a great secret and all of the soldiers of the *6.Panzerarmee* were ordered to strip the cuff titles with the name of their unit from their uniforms and each was assigned a cover name: the *Leibstandarte* thus became the *SS-Ersatzstaffel "Totenkopf"* and *6.Panzerarmee* became *Höherer Pionierführer Ungarn*.

Before leaving for Hungary, the units of the *Leibstandarte* were assembled in the Bonn-Euskirchen-Siegburg-Cologne region. The rail convoys with the division's vehicles and personnel passed through central Germany, Saxony, Bohemia and Moravia, Vienna, then to offload at Raab (Györ in Hungarian). On 30 January, *Heeresgruppe Süd*, to which *6.Panzerarmee* was subordinated, identified the Venek-Asvànyraro-Dunaszeg-Györ sector as the unloading area for the *Leibstandarte*. On 6 February a new order extended that

SS-Obstgruf. Joseph "Sepp" Dietrich.

SS-Ostubaf. Heinz von Westerhagen.

A King Tiger on the Hungarian front, 1945.

area towards Sondorf, the *Reich* frontier, St.Johann, Gyorsovénzhàz, Enese and the area to the north of Györ. As soon as they arrived in Hungary, the various units of the *Leibstandarte* received new recruits to replace the losses suffered in the Ardennes. Nevertheless only one unit was reorganized with trained personnel: the *I./SS-Pz.Rgt.1*, which received as reinforcements the crews without tanks of *II./SS-Pz.Rgt.1*, who had not taken part in the Ardennes offensive and had remained in reserve at Rahden. Thus, *SS-Ostuf.* Werner Wolff and *SS-Hstuf.* Heinz Malkomes arrived to replace *SS-Ustuf.* Hennecke and *SS-Ostuf.* Christ to lead the *1.* and *2.Kompanie*. With respect to the tank situation, on hand were twenty-one PzKpfw IV, twenty-five PzKpfw V and nineteen PzKpfw VI. Many other tanks were still under repair.

The *s.SS-Pz.Abt.501*, commanded by *SS-Ostubaf.* Westerhagen, re-equipped with the new Tiger II or King Tiger, had in the meantime been permanently integrated into the divisional structure.

Since late January 1945, *SS-Ostubaf.* Peiper had been transferred to Himmler's headquarters at Birkenwald, in the Prenzlau forest north of Berlin. On 4 February Peiper had his last meeting with the *Reichsführer-SS*. A few days later, he was transferred to the *SS-Panzergrenadierschule* at Kienschlag (Prosetschnitz) in the Protectorate of Bohemia and Moravia. On 14 February he left the school to return to the *Leibstandarte*.

Panzergruppe Peiper

The new German offensive on the Hungarian front designated in code as *Frühlingserwachen* (Spring Awakening), called for a maneuver along three routes in order to trap and destroy the Soviet forces located on the western bank of the Danube, after which the German forces were to continue east and liberate Budapest. The *III.Pz.Korps* of *Armeegruppe Balck* and Dietrich's *6.Panzerarmee*, moving from the area between Lake Balaton and Lake Velencze, were to reach the Danube near Dunaföldvar. The *2.Pz.Armee* under de Angelis was to attack from the south of Lake Balaton, between the Drava and Balaton itself and then move east towards the Danube (Operation "*Eisbrecher*"). The *16.SS-Pz.Gr.Div. "Reichsführer"*, attached to the *XII.Geb.Korps* was to advance from the Nagykanisza area, passing through Kaposvàr. *Heeresgruppe E* (from the Balkan front) was to move between Esseg and Miholjac, pushing to the northeast towards Mohàcs on the Drava (Operation "*Waldteufel*"). As of 1 February

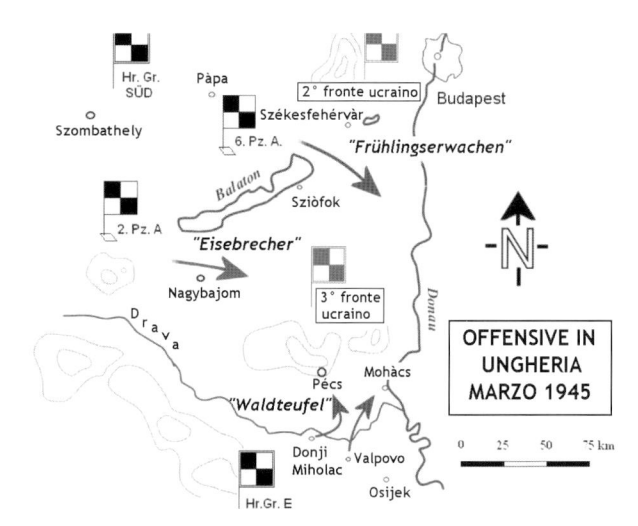

Planned routes of the German offensive in Hungary, 1945.

SS-Ostubaf. Rudolf Lehmann.   *SS-Staf,* Otto Kumm.

King Tiger on the Hungarian front, February 1945.

1945, only six convoys of the *Leibstandarte*, with elements of *SS-Pz.Rgt.1* and of the headquarters staff, had reached Hungary. As of 8 February, the operational status of armored vehicles of the *Leibstandarte* was as follows: 21 PzKpfw IV, 34 PzKpfw V, 15 PzKpfw VI and 8 Jg.Pz. IV. On 10 February, the chief of staff of *I.SS-Pz.Korps, SS-Ostubaf.* Rudolf Lehmann, was ordered to report to headquarters of *Heeresgruppe Süd*, where he received the following instructions: "*...The combat-ready elements of* I.SS-Pz.Korps *must move to the sector of the* 211.Volksgrenadier-Division. *The mission*

German tanks on the Hungarian plain.

February 1945: SS-Ostubaf. Peiper, on the left, discussing final details of the offensive with his unit commanders.

is to clean out the enemy bridgehead northwest of Gran, attacking with the 46.Inf.Div. and the bulk of 211.Volks. Gr.Div. and of the 44.RGD "HuD"…". The next day a new meeting was held, at which the difficulty of having the Panther and Tiger tanks to cross the Danube were brought up, as there was only one bridge available at Komàrom. It was then asked to organize the move of the tanks by train, to speed up the move and to save fuel. The move of *I.SS-Pz.Korps* and the assembly of *Pz.Korps "Feldherrnnhalle"* continued during the day of 12 February. During the night of 13 February, the unloading of the tracked elements of *I.SS-Pz.Korps began*. On 15 February, *SS-Brigdf.* Otto Kumm[22] assumed command of the *Leibstandarte*, busying himself with the formation of assault groups of the division with the elements that had already arrived in the sector and in function of the assigned objectives. It was to that end that an *Infanterie-Gruppe* was formed, led by *SS-Staf.* Max Hansen, consisting of elements of *SS-Pz.Gr.Rgt.1* and *2*, of *SS-Pz.Aufkl.-Abt.1*, two batteries of *SS-Flak-Abt.1* and a company of *SS-Pz.Jg.-Abt.1* under *SS-Hstuf.* Holst. At the same time, a *Panzergruppe* was created, commanded by *SS-Ostubaf.* Joachim Peiper with the *I.(gemischte) Abteilung*[23], the *s.SS-Pz.Abt.501*, the *III. (gep.)/2* and elements of *SS-Pz.Art.-Rgt.1*. Most of the division was still in a transfer status. On 16 February, on the eve of the offensive, bad weather continued to reign over the entire region, inundating fields and transforming the roads into enormous overflowing quagmires.

Operation Südwind

At dawn on 17 February, according to plan, the *Pz.Korps "FHH"* began its attack. On the right, the *44.Reichs-Grenadier-Division "HuD"* ran into stiff enemy resistance west of Nemetszögyen, while on the left, troops of the *46.Inf.Division* were able to surprise the Soviets, breaking through their lines between Nemetszögyen and Bart. The *"Feldherrnhalle"* armored group then joined in the action, moving from its positions to the south of Fartad, in support of the *"HuD"*, enabling it to push along the woods to the southwest of Nemetszögyen. *Panzergruppe Pei*per also began to move, as recounted by *SS-Ostuf.* Rolf Reiser, platoon leader in *1.Kp./SS-Pz.Rgt.1*[24]: *"…At dawn, the time came for us to move, following the army infantry division that had begun to march, in order to break through the Soviet main line of resistance. The road and ground conditions were bad.*

---

[22] Otto Kumm, born on 1 October 1909 in Hamburg, SS Number 18.727. He had served previously in *I./Sta. "Germania"* (1934), as commander of *2./Sta. "Deutschland"* (1938), of *III./"Der Führer"* (1940) and of *SS-Pz.Gr.Rgt. "Der Führer"* (1940). On 20 April 1943, promoted to the rank of *SS-Staf.*, he was transferred to *V.SS-Gebirgs-Korps* as chief of staff. On 1 February 1944, he assumed command of *7.SS-Frw.-Geb.-Div. "Prinz Eugen"*. On 9 November 1944 he was promoted to the rank of *SS-Brigadeführer*. He had been awarded the German Cross in Gold on 1 December 1941, with the Knight's Cross 16 February 1942, with the Oak Leaves on 6 April 1943 and with the Swords on 17 March 1945.

[23] The *1./Kp.* under *SS-Ostuf.* Wolff had 12 PzKpfw V, the *2.Kp.* under *SS-Hstuf.* Malkomes had 13 PzKpfw V, the *6.Kp.* under *SS-Ostuf.* Sternebeck had 10 PzKpfw IV and the *7.Kp.* under *SS-Hstuf.* Kilingelhöfer had 11 PzKpfw IV. In *s.SS-Pz.Abt.501*, the *1.Kp.* had 6 Tiger II, the *2.Kp.* had 14 Tiger II and the *3.Kp.* had 14 Tiger II.

[24] Ralf Tiemann, *Die Leibstandarte, Vol.IV/2*, pages 235-236.

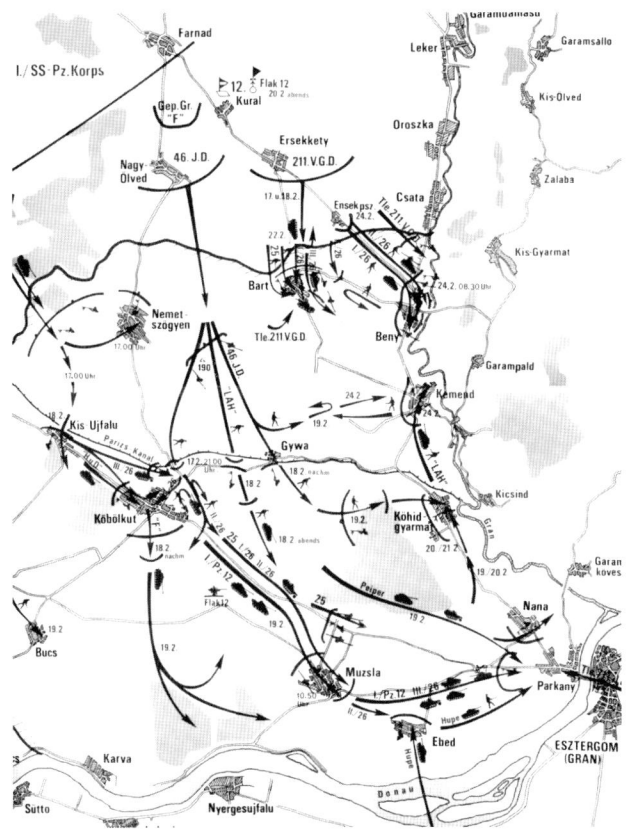

German unit movements during *Südwind*.

SS Panthers and King Tigers moving to attack.

Panzergruppe Peiper tanks and half-tracks moving forward. (Charles Trang)

PzKpfw IV in combat on the Hungarian front, 1945.

SS grenadiers in a trench, waiting for the tanks to pass, then to follow them in an attack against enemy positions.

A Panther during a pause, before resuming its attack.

***SS-Ustuf**. Günther Borchers aboard his Panther.*

An SS armored group moving to attack, February 1945.

The fields and meadows were inundated with water and the panzers were able to move only with difficulty in that immense bog. The 1.Kompanie *took the lead, then shifted to the right wing to provide cover for our attack zone. We continued along the road and advanced rapidly. Then, we passed in front of the former main line of resistance and stopped in a fold in the ground. Meanwhile, a mortar round exploded far behind us. After a brief meeting with Peiper, Poetschke and Diefenthal, we resumed out advance. The battalion deployed for the attack to the left of the road that led to Nem.Sedlin. We thus began to move forward, echeloned in depth, forming a large triangle. Marching with my platoon, on the right wing in a position to the rear, I was charged with covering the flank. We began to take fire from anti-tank guns as we approached Nem.Sedlin. When the moment came to pass in front of that village, we proceeded rapidly. We stopped soon after, behind a hill that was in front of us, preparing for the attack. There, we began to come under violent fire from mortars and "Stalin Organs". The Soviets must have spotted our assembly area. After having been joined by the SPW of* III.(gep.)/SS-Pz.Gren.Rgt.2 *and the grenadiers of* SS-Pz.Gr.Rgt.1, *the* Kampfgruppe *launched a determined attack against the objective of the day: the Pariszky Canal. With the Panthers and Tigers in the lead, followed by the Panzer.IVs and by the SPW half-tracks, we got over the hill and immediately*

Leibstandarte half-tracks on the march, February 1945.

Grenadiers and SPW of *III.(gep.)/2* during a pause.

A PzKpfw IV crossing a river in Hungary, 1945.

A group of PzKpfw IV in combat.

responded to the massive fire of the Soviet anti-tank guns. Thanks to our concentrated fire and our armored attack made without holding back the reins, we were able to overrun the anti-tank gun line and to throw the Soviets out of their positions. The enemy fled in the face of the fury of our attack. As night fell, our offensive thrust had reached as far as the canal, near Giwa, but the bridge over the river had been blown up!".

Regarding this attack, let us also hear the account by *SS-Sturmann* Reinhold Kyriss, of the 6.Pz.Kp.[25]: *Around noon, the* Panzergruppe *assembled for an attack against a position on the other side of the slope. The mission was clear. We were to pass across the front of a solid anti-tank screen.* SS-Ostubaf. *Peiper took the time to cover his flank, and it was a good thing. Peiper ordered five* Königstigers *to position themselves on the crest of the hill, as a target for the Soviet anti-tank guns. You could see the rounds bounce off the front armor of the King Tigers. It was a bad time for the Soviets when the Tigers began to return fire, destroying the anti-tank guns one after another. When the anti-tank fire ceased, Peiper gave the order: "…Panzer Marsch!" The panzers and the SPW moved ahead at full speed, firing with all of their weapons…It was an impressive scene. In the face of this armored attack, organized like a cavalry charge, the Soviets could do only one thing: run!* Kampfgruppe Peiper *suffered no losses during this attack"*. *Panzergruppe Peiper* and *46.Inf.Division*, attacking together, had reached the northern bank of the Pariszky Canal, on both sides of the Gywa (Sarka). In the meantime, *Kampfgruppe Hansen*, which had arrived to support the *46.Inf.Division*, followed it in its advance. The men of the *12.SS-Pz.Div. "Hitlerjugend"* in turn followed those of the *Leibstandarte*, crossing the main line of resistance during the evening. On the left, that is, on the eastern flank, units of *211.Volks.Gr.Div.* were heavily engaged on both sides of Bart, against battle-hardened Soviet troops.

During the night between 17 and 18 February, Hansen's men and those of *46.Inf.Div.* were able to establish a bridgehead on the canal, in the Sarka area. At dawn, they resumed their attacks, managing to expand it. Around noon, and after the engineers had been able to build bridges across the canal, the *Panzergruppe* resumed its advance, crossing through Särkanyfalva to reach the hills of Libad and Bela. Soon after, it was able to cross the Köbolkut-Parkany road. The armored units assumed defensive positions for the night.

---

[25] P. Agte, *Jochen Peiper, Commander Panzerregiment Leibstandarte*, page 512.

SS officers discussing an action.

An SS half-track on the edge of a Hungarian village in flames.

SS grenadiers behind a King Tiger during an attack.

SS-Ustuf. Günther Borchers, of the *9.(Pi.)Kp./ SS-Pz.Rgt.1*, describes this last attack[26]: "*...It was a tank attack like the old days. Königstiger, Panthers and SPW moved towards the enemy positions without being able to be stopped. The leading vehicles fell victim to mines. Firing to both sides, the mines were neutralized and we were able to continue. Szögyenm, Bator-Keszi, Köbölut, Muszla and another village were seized. The local populace welcomed us cordially, after having suffered Soviet occupation. Women of all ages had been barbarously violated by the enemy soldiers...*".

On 19 February, thanks to an improvement in the weather conditions, the *I.SS-Pz.Korps*, along with the *Regimentsgruppe "Hupe"*, was ordered to force a passage at Muszla and to capture the positions at Parkany and Nana. The armored groups of both of the SS divisions were sent forward, employing the *Panzerkeil* tactic, the armored wedge, with individual tanks deployed in a wedge formation at intervals of a hundred meters between each other, in order to protect themselves and to provide mutual support in case of need. With the Tigers and Panthers in the lead, every Soviet tank or anti-tank gun that tried to halt the German advance was reduced to silence by their devastating firepower. In the early afternoon, the armored spearheads moved to the north to hit the positions of the 4th Guards Corps, dug in on the western bank of the Gran River. The *Leibstandarte's Panzergruppe* reached the Parkany

---

[26] Ibidem, page 513.

road, where it was attacked by Soviet fighter-bombers, incurring new losses. In the meantime, *III.(gep.)/2* moved towards nana, capturing it with the support of tanks from *6.Kp./SS-Pz.Rgt.1*. Thanks to the successes achieved during the day, the German command decided to regroup the *Leibstandarte* units and throw them against Kam.Darmoty from the south.

On 20 February, Peiper decided to attack with the aid of dusk to protect the armored assault groups from enemy artillery fire; the panzers went on the attack by the light of luminous flares and by the flames that rose from the hulks of knocked-out enemy tanks, towards Kam.Darmoty. Not all of the panzers took part in the attack, because of lack of fuel. It was mainly the PzKpfw IV of the *6.* and *7.Kp.* that advanced on both sides of the Parkany-Kemend road. At the first light of dawn, despite getting off to a good start, the attack was completely halted before Kam.Darmoty by a violent artillery barrage unleashed by the Soviet artillery, coming from the eastern bank of the Gran River. In the afternoon, *Kampfgruppe Hansen* set up defensive positions outside of the city. During the night of 21 February, *Panzergruppe Peiper* arrived to support Hansen's men, to make a fresh attack against Kam.Darmoty. The *46.Inf. Div.* also attacked, moving from the west. Let us read the testimony of Rolf Reiser regarding this new fighting[27]: "…SS-Standartenführer *Peiper had decided to make a night attack because by day we were incessantly targeted by enemy artillery fire, located on the eastern bank. Only five tanks of 1.Kompanie were still operational. We thus began to move towards Kam.Darmoty. Enemy artillery at first began to make itself heard, attempting to block our way. Once we had gotten close to that locality, we turned to the east, in order to be able to infiltrate from the front. At that point the enemy artillery intensified its fire. A wall of steel and fire fell upon us. Flares and tracers lit up the night, pointing the way to the enemy positions. We wanted to get through this barrier by moving rapidly. It was at full speed that we broke into this destructive fire. Our tracks screeched on the railway tracks…we were hit, without knowing if it was by an enemy tank, an anti-tank gun or direct artillery fire. The tank began to burn. It was not necessary to give an order to bail out of the tank, but it was necessary to traverse the turret that was blocking the driver's hatch…*". It was not until 21:00 that the *Panzergruppe* succeeded in capturing the position of Kam.Darmoty, with the support of the infantrymen of *46.Inf.Div.*, while *6.Panzerkompanie* was engaged inside Köhidgyarmat. On 22 February the *Leibstandarte*, the *46.Inf.Div.* and the "HuD" Division continued their sweep operations along the western bank of the Gran. The Soviets continued to

Leibstandarte officers discussing their orders.

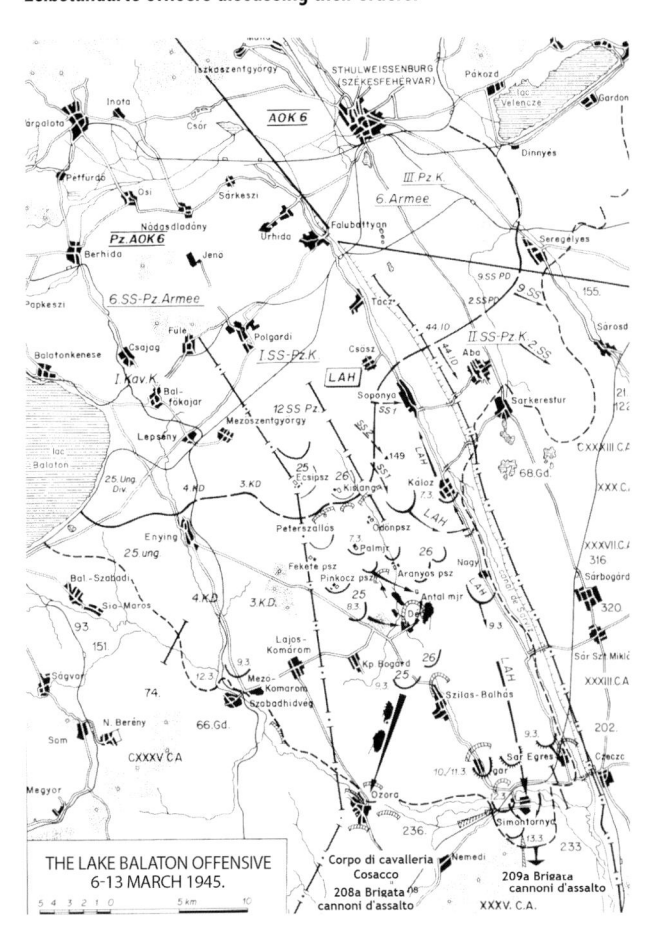

THE LAKE BALATON OFFENSIVE 6-13 MARCH 1945.

stubbornly defend their positions, without skimping on men or ammunition. An armored *Kampfgruppe* of the *Leibstandarte*, consisting of elements of *1.SS-Pz.Art.-Rgt.1* and of *III.(gep.)/2*, pushed northwards, to ensure control of the crossroads between Kemend and Kam.Darmoty.

In the meantime, troops to the *12.SS-Pz.Div. "HJ"* had taken the position at Bart. The *8.Armee* then decided to assemble the two divisions of *1.SS-Pz.Korps*, to make a new attack to eliminate what remained of the bridgehead in the Bina area. The *Leibstandarte* was to attack from the

---

[27] P.Agte, *Jochen Peiper, Commander Panzerregiment Leibstandarte*, page 517.

south and the *Hitlerjugend* from the northwest. Seeking to limit losses caused by enemy artillery fire from the eastern bank of the Gran, it was decided to launch an attack on the night of the 24th: at 2:00, troops from the *Leibstandarte* attacked from the south, while troops of the "*HuD*" Division and the *46.Inf.Div.* attacked from the southwest. The *12.SS-Pz.Division* and the *211. Volksgrenadier-Division* were to attack Bina from the north and west. After the destruction of the bridges over the Gran River, the fighting ceased soon after noontime. At the same time, the position at Bina was taken by units of the *Hitlerjugend* after a furious battle. The Soviets withdrew from the Gran bridgehead, after having taken heavy losses; more than two thousand dead, six thousand wounded and five hundred prisoners. On 25 February, *Leibstandarte* troops began to leave the Gran sector to reassemble north of Komàrom. From there, on 1 March, they began to move to the Veszprem-Osku-Nagyesztergar-Bakonytamasi-Csot-Bakonybel-Marko area, for the imminent new offensive at Lake Balaton. It was there that Peiper presented the last awards to his men. On the eve of the new attack, the *Leibstandarte* had three *Panzergrenadier* battalions at full manning, one battalion almost fully manned, and the other three at half manning. The tank situation within the SS division at that moment was as follows: fourteen PzKpfw IV, twenty-six PzKpfw V and fifteen Jg.Pz. V.

Operation Frühlingserwachen

After having eliminated the bridgehead on the Gran, the German forces were able to prepare to launch Operation "Spring Awakening", moving to the south: 220,000 men and about 320 tanks, assault guns and tank destroyers attacked on 6 March 1945. The *Schw-*

March 1945: A group of Panthers from *I./SS-Pz.Rgt.1* on the march. (Ullstein Bild)

Hungary, March 1945: An SdKfz.251 Ausf.D and a PzKpfw IV of the 6.Kp., followed by other SdKfz.251 of *Panzergrippe Peiper*.

Assault guns moving through the mud and water to reach the front line.

SS grenadiers. (Charles Trang)

88

erpunkt, the focal point of the attack, was concentrated between lakes Balaton and Velencze, with the *6.Panzerarmee* in the vanguard and Gille's *IV.SS-Pz.Korps* protecting its left flank. For the first time, six *Waffen SS* armored divisions were fighting together. The surprise effect, however, went up in smoke: the presence of the *SS-Pz.Korps* in Hungarian territory during the earlier Operation *Südwind* had alerted the Soviet commands to the imminence of a new German offensive in the short term. The *Stavka* had accordingly ordered an immediate and massive reinforcement of the defenses in the area of Lake Balaton, south of Budapest and the construction of a system of deep field fortifications with minefields, anti-tank gun positions and deep ditches. The advance of German units was also stalled by mud and numerous streams on the Hungarian plain. The operation began officially at 04:30 on 6 March 1945; the *Leibstandarte* units attacked without any preparatory artillery fire, in an attempt to surprise the Soviets. In the preceding days, the rain had fallen without letup and the entire Hungarian plain had become an enormous bog; despite the mud, Siebken's grenadiers of *SS-Pz.Gr.Rgt.2* had succeeded in making it through a minefield and capturing Hill 149, a hill that dominated all of the ground northeast of Kislang. At the same time, *Panzergruppe Poetschke* had been stalled after having advanced two kilometers to the west of Hill 149. It had also lost a large number of vehicles to mines. *SS-Pz.Gr.Rgt.1* made its attack later, due to the delay with which it had reached its departure point. In the evening, it was able to capture a large part of Soponya. In the other sectors of the offensive, the situation was certainly no better: troops of the *12.SS-Pz.Div. "Hitlerjugend"* were quickly halted after some initial success, the *II.Kavallerie-Korps* had been thrown back to its departure positions by an enemy counterattack and units of *II.SS-Pz.Korps* managed only towards evening to reach their assembly area, having to postpone the beginning of their attack until the following day. Southwest of Lake Balaton, the *2.Panzerarmee* had not achieved any worthwhile results. On the other hand, *Heeresgruppe* E had succeeded in crossing the Drava and establishing two bridgeheads and *III.Pz.Korps* had been able to occupy a large part of Seregelyes, south of Lake Velencze. On 17 March, *Leibstandarte* units resumed their attack to the southeast, continuing to march in the mud; after having reached the Kaloz area, the continued on to the east, to cut the Kaloz-Simontornya road. The Kaloz position was taken shortly thereafter.

On 8 March, the SS troops continued to advance: *SS-Pz.Gr.Rgt.1* was busy clearing out the Sopnya sec-

A Flakpanzer IV *"Wirbelwind"*.

A Panther moving through a Hungarian village, March 1945.

A King Tiger on the Hungarian front, March 1945.

A *I.SS-Pz.Korps* Panther heading to the front line.

tor, while *SS-Pz.Gr.Rgt.2*, after having been withdrawn from its positions south of Kaloz, succeeded in eliminating an anti-tank front and capture the position at Nagyhörcsok Puszta. Attacking from the southwest, the *I./2* captured intact a bridge over the Maldom, crossed the river and found itself facing a new anti-tank front to the south and southwest of Nagyhörcsok. This enemy position was eliminated after a furious battle. Peiper's *Panzergruppe* followed the movements of *SS-Pz.Gr.Rgt.2*, capturing the hills north of Nagyhörcsok. Enemy resistance stiffened northwest of that location and in the afternoon a ferocious firefight ensued between German panzers and Soviet anti-tank guns.

On 9 March, thanks to the improved weather conditions, the SS troops made a massive attack, employing *SS-Pz.Gr.Rgt.2* and the *Panzergruppe* directed towards Simontornya, and *SS-Pz.Gr.Rgt.1, SS-Pz.Aufkl.-Abt.1* and *SS-Pz.Jg.-Abt.1* towards Sar Egres. The *Panzergruppe* reached the hills near Janos Major, where its tanks clashed with a *Pakfront*, suffering enemy artillery fire coming from the southern bank of the River Sio. Around noontime, the *Panzergruppe* had to set up defensive positions in front of Simontornya. Let us hear the testimony of *SS-Oberscharführer* Kurt Fickert, *Flak* platoon leader in *4.Kp./SS-Pz.Abt.501*: *"...We were positioned behind the Tigers and Panthers to eliminate the enemy infantry. I had received from Peiper the order to support our grenadiers in the fighting in the streets. A few Panthers followed us to destroy the enemy tanks that approached. I had been assigned two of* SS-Ostuf. *Vogler's* Wirbelwinds. *Most of the Tiger II tanks were out of action because of problems with their differentials.* SS-Ostubaf. *Peiper had prohibited us from firing against enemy aircraft. It was important to protect our infantry and we had to save our ammunition for combat against ground targets"*.

On 10 March, while the men of the *23.Pz.Division*, called upon to reinforce the *I.SS-Pz.Korps*, were blocked by Soviet artillery fire, the *Leibstandarte* continued its attacks towards Sar Egres and Simontornya, despite the fact that Soviet resistance had become even stronger.

An SS grenadier sheltering alongside a PzKpfw IV.

An SS Panther commander.

Waffen SS troops in a Hungarian village and an SdKfz.251 on the move.

An SS SdKfz.251.

SS grenadiers advancing, bypassing the hulks of destroyed vehicles.

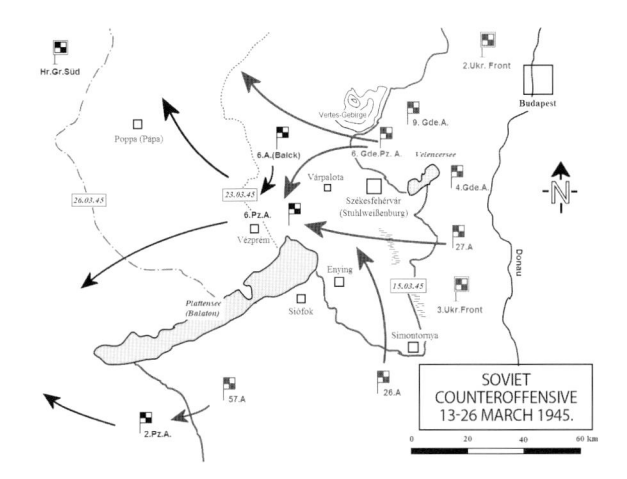

Soviet tanks and infantry moving to attack, March 1945.

According to testimony by Adam Rensch, of *7.Kp./2*, the *Panzergruppe* succeeded in attacking a village near Simontornya, but the *7.Kp.2*. which was supposed to escort it, was not able to follow it at the same speed and this allowed the crews of the enemy tank destroyers to hold off the panzers. *SS-Ostubaf*. Peiper called his commander, *SS-Ostuf*. Kübler, on the carpet, threatening him with a court martial because of his failure to support the fighting that had taken place in the village.

Kübler was later killed in front of Sar Egres and his company's 3rd Platoon was completely wiped out that same day. The *Leibstandarte* was engaged in repelling the violent counterattacks by Soviet tanks and infantry. The position at Simontornya was solidly defended by anti-tank guns and by anti-aircraft batteries. At least two PzKpfw IV of *6.Kp./SS-Pz.Rgt.1* were knocked out during the course of subsequent attacks.

On 11 March, the men of the division continued to fight before Simontornya, without however being able to gain any ground. Fortunately for them, to their right, the *12.SS-Pz.Div. "Hitlerjugend"* had succeeded in seizing the position at Igar, which allowed their exposed flank to be covered. The *Leibstandarte* infantry units and *SS-Pz.Gr.Rgt.26* of the *Hitlerjugend* led by *SS-Stubaf*. Kostenbader were engaged together to seize the crossroads north of Simontornya. *SS-Ustuf*. Hermann Gerdes[28] of the *2.Pz.Kp.* then tried to take advantage of the darkness to make a raid with the three Panthers of his platoon. Two tanks were knocked out by enemy fire on the plain outside of Simontornya; even though he was now alone, *SS-Ustuf*. Gerdes managed to reach the bridge over the Sio. In order to avoid any risk, the Soviets blew the bridge and soon after also tried to knock out Gerdes' Panther. However, the SS officer was able to fend off their attacks, passing the night between the enemy lines.

On the morning of 12 March, the *6.Pz.Kp.* attacked towards Simontornya; without stopping to fire, moving rapidly, the PzKpfw IV reached the western edge of the village, then pushed through the streets to the east and to the south. There were brief but intense clashes. In

---

[28] Ralf Tiemann, *Die Leibstandarte*, Vol.IV/2, page 323.

the end, Simontornya was captured, but five PzKpfw IV had been destroyed. At the same time, the SS engineers had succeeded in establishing a bridgehead on the Sio River, attacking aboard motorized rubber rafts. During the night, the grenadiers of *SS-Pz.Gr.Rgt.1* (*LSSAH*) and of *SS-Pz.Gr.Rgt.26* (*Hitlerjugend*) crossed to the southern bank of the river.

On 13 March, *SS-Pz.Gr.Rgt.26* was able to capture Hill 220, which dominated the entire sector, while the engineers were building a bridge across the river, which allowed the first tanks to cross.

On 14 March, taking advantage of improved weather conditions, Soviet aviation heavily attacked the *I.SS-Pz. Korps* positions. At the same time, violent ground attacks were made against the positions of *SS-Pz.Gr.Rgt.1* and *SS-Pz.Gr.Rgt.26*, all of which were driven off with heavy losses for the Soviets. Around noontime, the two SS regiments took Hill 115, two kilometers south of Simontornya, in an attempt to enlarge the bridgehead. Soviet artillery then began heavily shelling the entire sector, destroying the bridge over the Sio that had been built by the SS engineers, making it necessary to build another further to the west. A *Kampfgruppe* of *SS-Pz. Gr.Rgt.2* and a *Panzergruppe*, consisting of *SS-Pz.Jg.Abt.1* and elements of *23.Panzer-Division*, successfully attacked the bridgehead over the Sarviz Canal, in the Czecze area, forcing the Soviet troops to withdraw to the opposite bank. In the meantime, German air reconnaissance had spotted strong Soviet troop concentrations further to the north, in the Szekesfehervar-Zamoly area, right in front of *IV.SS-Pz.Korps*, a sign that the Soviets were preparing to launch a massive offensive against the rear of *6.Panzerarmee*. At that point, *SS-Obstgruf.* Sepp Dietrich had to decide whether to continue the attacks south of the Sio or to halt them, in order to deal with this new threat. And it was thus that, during the course of the evening, most of *SS-Pz.Rgt.1* and *s.SS-Pz.Abt.501* were withdrawn from the front line and transferred to the Deg sector.

On 15 March, while the *Kampfgruppen* of *SS-Pz. Gr.Rgt.*1 continued to fight to enlarge the bridgehead to

Panther tanks moving through a Hungarian village.

Soviet infantry attacking, supported by tanks.

Grenadiers armed with *Panzerfaust*, March 1945.

Grenadiers and StuG.III in a defensive position.

the south, Sepp Dietrich sought authorization to be able to withdraw his army in order to avoid having his divisions cut off south of lakes Balaton and Velencze by the impending new Soviet offensive. Headquarters of *Heeresgruppe Süd* then decided to forestall the Soviet offensive with an immediate counterattack made by the armored forces of *6.Armee* and *6.Panzerarmeee* between the Sarviz Canal and Lake Velencze, towards the crossings over the Danube. To that end, the *I.SS-Pz.Korps* divisions had to be assembled in the rear areas of *II.SS-Pz.Korps* and *III. Pz.Korps*. In the night, around 23:00, the order was issued for *I.SS-Pz.Korps* to withdraw from its positions.

The Soviet counteroffensive

On 16 March, the Soviets launched their offensive between Lake Velencze and Bicske, in the sector defended by Gille's *IV.SS-Pz.Korps*. The 3rd Ukrainian front made its main effort between Szekesfehervar and Tatabanya, rapidly threatening Komàrom and succeeding in splitting *6.Armee* in two, at the boundary between the Hungarian 2nd Armored Division and the *3.SS-Pz. Div. "Totenkopf"*. Weather conditions were now good and the sun had dried the roads, allowing the Soviet units to move rapidly. General Guderian ordered the

SS-Ostuf. Werner Wolff. (NA)

An SS defensive position in Hungary, with an 81mm mortar.

A Jagdpanzer IV engaged against Soviet tanks, March 1945.

SS grenadiers deployed along a stretch of railway line.

immediate withdrawal of *I.SS-Pz.Korps* to the north, as suggested by Dietrich himself. Hitler did not give his approval until 18 March, causing more time to be lost. The objective was to make a counterattack in the Varpalota area, against Zamoly, in order to try to cut off the Soviet vanguard from their rear area. It was thus not until the night of 18 March that the withdrawal of the forces engaged south of the Sio Canal began to withdraw. The bridge at Simontornya fell under the weight of a panzer while it was crossing, further slowing the northward movement of the troops.

Most of *SS-Pz.Rgt.1* was at Janoshaza and was able to reach the Deg-Enying sector without any problem at around 18:00. At that time the *Panzergruppe* had sixteen panzers still operational and another thirty-eight undergoing repair. The move to the north took place under increasingly difficult conditions, because the roads were full of columns of civilians who were fleeing the Soviet hordes.

On 19 March, the Soviets pressed their attacks on the Vertes massif, to the north and northwest of Szekesfehervar, where the 9th and 6th Guards Armies continued to push towards Varpalota. Their forward elements had already reached the area that had been designated as the assembly area for the *Leibstandarte*, whose advance guard had to fight to disengage. Around 16:00 the *Panzergruppe* reached the sector, but the situation continued to be confused. During the night, the Soviets attacked the city once again. The orders for *6.Panzerarmee* were at all costs to prevent the enemy breaking through between Lake Velencze and Mor, and between Környe as far as the area to the east of Esztergom. Once the situation had stabilized, the SS troops were to attack

SS grenadiers, despite strong enemy pressure. In the afternoon, *Kampfgruppe Sternebeck*, with six PzKpfw IV of the *6.Kp./SS-Pz.Rgt.1* and two Tigers of *1.Kp./s.SS-Pz.Abt.501*, was cut off to the east of Inota. Sternebeck had no contact with Peiper's command post. From his position, he could see that Inota was in flames, under Soviet artillery fire. That meant that the city had fallen into enemy hands. Sternebeck then decided to gamble it all, attacking. Throughout that day, seventy-six Soviet tanks were knocked out, nineteen of which by *7.Kp./SS-Pz.Rgt.1*. *SS-Uscha*. Clotten personally destroyed six. During the fighting, *SS-Ostuf*. Werner Wolff was

SS grenadiers sheltering in a trench.

SS-Brigdf. Kumm, on the left, discussing the situation with other officers.

the Szekesfehervar-Vertes Mountain line, towards the east, to wipe out and push back the Soviet forces and finally to protect the Danube crossings at Komàrom and the petroleum refineries to the east of that city. For the following day, *I.SS-Pz.korps* was assigned the mission to secure the assembly area from where its counterattack was to jump off and to counterattack towards the heights located east of Csor, to the west of Fehervarcsurgo and Bodajk. At the same time it was necessary to block the enemy advance northwest of Szkesfehervar.

On 20 March, at 4:00, the *Leibstandarte* attacked the enemy armored formations that were in the Varpalota area, committing all of the tanks and tanks destroyers it had available. About thirty T-34 tanks were destroyed, but that did not stop the Soviets. On the right flank, to the north of the Inota-Szekesfehervar railway line, near Reti Puszta and near Csor, the attack of the SS troops was stopped by the strong superiority of the Soviets. On the left flank, the fighting was equally tough, but there were primarily infantry units there. The position at Tès was stubbornly defended by the

An SS grenadier launching a grenade with his Mauser rifle.

94

badly wounded; hit by a splinter from a mortar round while he was slightly exposed from the turret of his tank to give orders; he was brought to the hospital at Götzendorf, where he died on 30 March 1945.

On 21 March, defensive combat continued. The *3.SS-Pz.Div. "Totenkopf"*, falling back from the north and northeast, was subordinated to the *I.SS-Pz.Korps* and was able forces to launch a new counterattack; in particular, *6.Panzerarmee* was to seal the gap that had been opened in the Osi-Varpalota sector, prepare an attack towards Kocs, and maintain the bridgehead south of the Danube. Execution of these orders naturally appeared impossible, considering the state in which Dietrich's divisions were in and that the bulk of the forces of Hermann Balck's

A *Waffen SS* half-track towing a bogged down truck while crossing one of the many streams on the Hungarian plain.

General Hermann Balck, commander of 6.Armee.

assigned to support the *Leibstandarte* at Varpalota. There, the Soviets attacked with three rifle divisions, but were pushed back by *Kampfgruppe Hansen*, which claimed the destruction of about fifteen tanks. Around noontime, the Soviets again attacked the city, from the east, north and southeast, strongly testing the SS units; another forty-six enemy tanks were knocked out during the defensive fighting. On the left flank, Siebken's *SS-Pz.Gr.Rgt.2* was completely cut off following a Soviet breakthrough, while it attempted to make contact with elements of the "*Hitlerjugend*". The *Kampfgruppen* of *SS-Pz.Gr.Rgt.2*, supported by the Jagdpanzer IV of *SS-Pz.Jg.-Abt.*1 and by the engineers of *SS-Pz.Pi.-Btl.1*, nevertheless were able to repel attacks by Soviet infantry to the west of Tès. The attacks by the 6th Guards Tank Army in the sector between Szekesfehervar, Varpalota and Bakony Csernye, prevented the *I.SS-Pz.Korps* from effectively deploying its forces in the field. It now appeared impossible that the SS corps could on its own halt an entire Soviet army over such a vast front. In the Szekesfehrvar sector, the *5.SS-Pz.Div. "Wiking"*, threated with being surrounded and being wiped out, was on the verge of abandoning the city. Nevertheless, that evening, the order came from *Heeresgruppe Süd* headquarters to assemble all of the avail-

Werner Poetschke, wearing the rank of *SS-Hstuf*.

6.Armee were surrounded south of Szekesfehervar and that their complete destruction had been avoided thanks to the defensive battles fought by the *Kampfgruppen* of the *Leibstandarte* and of the *Hohenstaufen*.

On 22 March, shortly after midnight, Szekesfehervar was abandoned by the troops of the *Wiking*. In the morning, the 6th Guards Tank Army resumed its offensive towards Veszprem. Its attack completely caught the *Leibstandarte's Panzergruppe* and elements of *SS-Pz.Gr.Rgt.1*, cutting them off from *Kampfgruppe Siebken*, consisting of *SS-Pz.Gr.Rgt.2*, *SS-Flak-Abt.1* and *SS-Pz.Jg.-Abt.1*, which was fighting to the west of Tés. *SS-Stubaf.* Poetschke was ordered to keep the road to Veszprem open. What was left of the *Panzergruppe* then began to march to the south, reaching Veszprem around 23:00.

On 23 March, the *Leibstandarte's* two main *Kampfgruppen* continued to fight separately, without any contact between them. On the left, Siebken's group was forcefully

Waffen SS troops withdrawing on the Hungarian front, March 1945.

An SS defensive position.

Waffen SS soldiers in a trench on the Hungarian plain.

Hungary, March 1945: Jagdpanther IV and grenadiers armed with Panzerfaust.

attacked from the east and southeast, while other Soviet armored formations sought to overrun his positions from the south. In the end, Siebken was forced to pull his forces back to the Lokut-Zirc line. In the meantime, on the right flank, most of *SS-Pz.Gr.Rgt.1*, the rest of the *Panzergruppe*, some elements of *SS-Flak-Abt.1* and of *SS-Pz.Jg.-Abt.1* were engaged in a furious and desperate battle at Veszprem. The city had to be abandoned to the Soviets shortly thereafter. Those forces engaged to the south, commanded by Otto Kumm, then came under the subordination of Hermann Balck's *6.Armee*. They withdrew to the north, towards Hajmasker and Kadarta, then towards evening, assumed a defensive stance in the area to the east of Marko.

Let us hear the testimony of Rolf Reiser regarding these latest encounters[29]: "...*it was around 6:00 in the morning when we crossed through Veszprem with nine panzers, some SPW and two* Schwimmwagen, *to go to take up positions on the edge of the city, towards the northeast. The place gave the impression of being deserted. From time to time we encountered isolated vehicles that travelled at high speed. I was in the lead with* SS-Stubaf. *Poetschke in a* Schwimmwagen *to reconnoiter the terrain in the eastern*

---
[29] Ralf Tiemann, *Die Leibstandarte. Vol.IV/2*, page 323.

SS troops pulling back, along a dried-up canal.

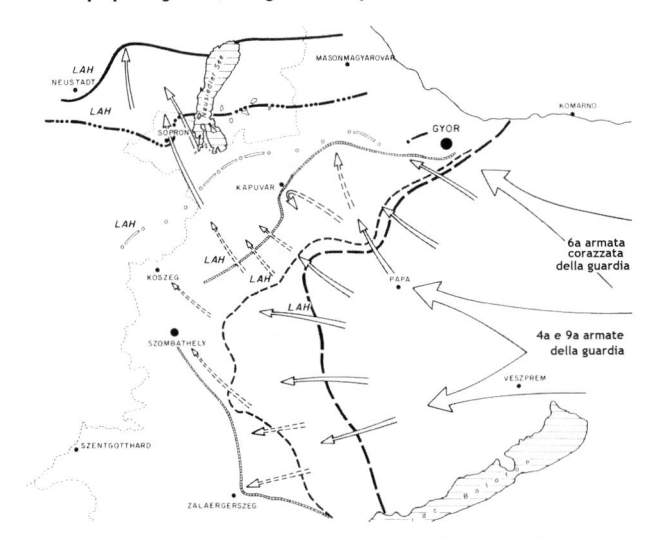

Routes of the Soviet offensive between 17 March and 2 April 1945.

A Soviet tank formation in a Hungarian village, 1945.

part of the city. The panzers followed. It was a cloudless day and it was already warm at that hour of the morning. We left the vehicle and crossed some gardens to get a better view of the ground that lay before us. With our binoculars we spotted an armored column that was moving from Kadarta with maybe thirty to forty tanks and that was approaching Veszprem, moving to the south. Our panzers had followed us and Poetschke gave the order to go and find all of the tank commanders as soon as possible, in order to bring them up to date. The group of commanders gathered near a haystack, all around Poetschke. Suddenly, a mortar round, by surprise, exploded right in the midst of the group. The consequences: SS-Stubaf. Poetschke was seriously wounded and died soon after[30]*, SS-Ustuf. Münkmeier, Gerdes and Heubeck and three other tank commanders were wounded more or less seriously. All however were no longer fit to fight. We did our best to aid the wounded. Despite his serious wound, Poetschke judged the situation to be desperate and shouted to SS-Ustuf. Pönisch, the communications officer: ...Transmit by radio to commander Peiper what's happening here!"* In addition, *SS-Ustuf.* Willi Stehle, Hubert Kaufmann and Heinz Rehagel, of the *1, 2. and 7.Kp./SS-Pz.Rgt.1* were also wounded during the fighting for Veszprem. This sudden lack of officers forced Peiper to reorganize the structure of *I.(gemischte)Abt./SS-Pz.Rgt.1*; all of the available Panthers were grouped under the command of *SS-Hstuf.* Ernst Otto, who until that time had commanded the *Versorgungs-Kp./SS-Pz.Rgt.1*. The Panzer IV were placed under the command of *SS-Hstuf.* Oskar Klingelhöfer, replaced in early April by *SS-Ostuf.* Werner Sternebeck.

Throughout the day of 24 March, the *6.Panzerarmee*, with its six divisions exhausted and with very depleted manning, continued to withdraw under the blows inflicted by four Soviet armies. Sepp Dietrich twice requested the return of the *Gruppe Süd* of the *Leibstandarte* to his army. But Balck took no measures in that respect, even though he had to defend a narrower front and having more forces at his disposal than Dietrich had. The *Gruppe Süd*, under Kumm's direct command, had to abandon its assembly area at Marko during the night between 23 and 24 March to avoid being surrounded, withdrawing first to Varöslod and then to Kislöd. In the latter location, *SS-Pz.Gr.Rgt.1* and the remnants of *SS-Pz.Rgt.1* succeeded in warding off an attack by Soviet forces pursuing them. The *III. (gep.)/2* took up defensive positions at Ajka, south of Kislöd and *SS-Pz.Aufkl.-Abt.1* to the east and southeast of Urkut. *Gruppe Nord* also, in contact on its left with men of the *12.SS-Pz.Div. "HJ"*, at risk of being surrounded, fell back to the line Kup-Papakovacsi-Ugod. That maneuver further widened the gap between the two main *Kampfgruppen* of the division. The Soviets took advantage of that to march on Papa. On the right, *Gruppe Süd* lost contact with the *3.Pz.Division* and the rest of *6.Armee*, and found itself completely cut off. The *6.Panzerarmee* finally authorized the relief of *Gruppe*

---

[30] Poetschke was badly wounded in his leg which was completely mangled. The battalion doctor, Doctor Neumayer,, proposed to amputate it, but Poetschke refused categorically, despite his situation deteriorating by the hour. He finally passed away in the early morning hours of 24 March. To the very end, he continued to repeat: *"If I can't serve in a tank any longer, then life no longer has any sense for me"*.

Soviet tanks with accompanying infantry, attacking.

Two soldiers help a wounded comrade.

Süd in order to enable it to attack to the northwest, re-establish contact with *Gruppe Nord*, and halt the advance of Soviet units outside of Tapocafö.

On 25 March, the Soviets launched a major new offensive, having as its objective Bratislava and Vienna. At the same time, north of the Danube, the *8.Armee* front was completely overrun. For the entire night, the two *Leibstandarte Kampfgruppen* managed to repel all of the Soviet attacks against their newly established positions. In the meantime, the *I.SS-Pz.Korps* had been ordered to cover the Papa sector with all available forces, in particular with *Gruppe Süd*, as soon as it was detached from *6.Armee*. Meanwhile, a large breach had been opened in the Ajka-Devecser sector which forced *Heeeresgruppe Süd* to order a withdrawal to the Marczal Canal.

On 26 March, the *Leibstandarte* attempted to stem Soviet progress, defending its positions along the line Noszlop-Kup-Papakovacsi. Around noon, on the right wing, the defenders at Noszlop were flanked from the south and were thus surrounded. *SS-Pz.Gr.Rgt.1* then had to open an escape route to the west and the Marczal Canal.

On 27 March, the *Leibstandarte's Panzergruppe* made one of its last counterattacks to try to fend off the advance of Soviet tanks in the Noszlop sector. The division had in any case to continue to withdraw towards the Raab River, which the Soviets had already reached in several places. The *Kampfgruppen* of *SS-Pz.Gr.Rgt.2* were engaged south of Kenyeri and those of *SS-Pz.Gr.Rgt.1* were busy defending the area northwest of Celldömök. Around noontime, they were forced to withdraw to new defensive positions on the western bank of the river. A bridgehead was kept in order to be able to save the last troops who had remained behind. In the afternoon, the Soviets succeeded in getting tanks and infantry troops onto the western bank of the river. Some panzers and *III.(gep.)/2* were engaged against them in the Niczk area.

On 28 March, starting from the bridgehead, the Soviets continued their attacks westward, meeting almost no resistance, making a movement to the northwest in order to envelop the right wing of the *Leibstandarte*. The SS troops had to give up the position at Jafka, in order to withdraw to strongpoints held by *SS-Pz.Gr.Rgt.2* along the Hegyfalu-Vamoscslad line.

On 29 March, the order was given to withdraw to the *Reichsschutzstellung*, the *Reich* protection line, known also as the *Südostwall*. The successive moves led the division to the Locs line (*SS-Pz.Gr.Rgt.1*)-Felsösag (*SS-Pz.Gr.Rgt.2*). The Soviet attacks were initially held at bay, but then during the day, the enemy broke through the *Reichsschutzstellung* to the north of Güns, entering into *Reich* territory.

On 30 March, *Leibstandarte* troops continued their retreat to the new line of resistance, continuing to fight strongly. The Soviets tried to exploit the twenty-five kilometer wide gap that separated *6.Armee* from *6.Panzerarmee*, in order to break through the new German defensive lines. In the Nikitisch sector, the Soviet spearheads were stalled by the *Kampfgruppen* of *SS-Pz.Rgt.1*. At the same time, troops of *SS-Pz.Rgt.2* were engaged in defensive fighting in the Löwö area, before pulling back to Sopronkövsed. The divisional logistical support units had in the meantime already pulled back behind the *Reichsschutzstellung*. On 31 March the *Leibstandarte* continued its withdrawal towards Wiener Neustadt. The divisional artillery redeployed its batteries south of Odenburg, on the other side of the *Reich* border.

Final combat in Austria

SS-Ostubaf. Peiper in Austria, April 1945.

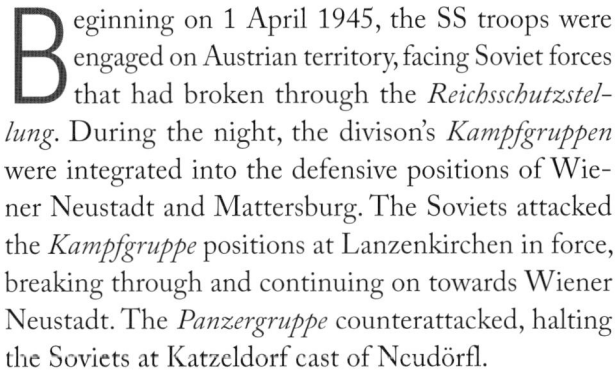

German troops retreating in Austria, 1945.

Peiper conferring with *SS-Ostubaf.* Martin Gross, commander of *SS-Pz. Rgt.12* of the *Hitlerjugend*.

Beginning on 1 April 1945, the SS troops were engaged on Austrian territory, facing Soviet forces that had broken through the *Reichsschutzstellung*. During the night, the divison's *Kampfgruppen* were integrated into the defensive positions of Wiener Neustadt and Mattersburg. The Soviets attacked the *Kampfgruppe* positions at Lanzenkirchen in force, breaking through and continuing on towards Wiener Neustadt. The *Panzergruppe* counterattacked, halting the Soviets at Katzeldorf east of Neudörfl.

On 2 April the forces of the 2nd and 3rd Ukrainian Fronts kicked off a new general offensive against the lines of *Heeresgruppe Süd. 2.Panzerarmee's* positions were quickly overrun and the defensive line pulled back along the course of the River Muir. The Soviet main effort was concentrated against the *6.Panzerarmee*, with the aim of reaching Vienna as soon as possible. To the left of the *Leibstandarte*, troops of *12.SS-Pz.Div. "Hitlerjugend"*, attacked by forces of the 6th Guards Army, fell back to Blumau and Leobersdorf. In the *Leibstandarte's* sector, the 6th Guards Tank Army captured Wiener Neustadt and continued its offensive northward, towards Kottingbrunn. The division's *Kampfgruppen* withdrew during the night to the west, taking up defensive positions at the entrance to the Piesting Valley, at the foot of the mountains east of Bad Fischau and Wöllersdorf, succeeding in establishing a continuous defensive front. The *Panzergruppe* did not reach Piesting until the late afternoon.

On 3 April, defensive fighting continued with greater intensity, especially in the area south of Vienna, where Soviet forces were making their main effort. The positions defended by *Leibstandarte* troops were attacked by tanks and infantry, particularly in the Bad Fischau area.

In the Piesting area as well, there was fresh fighting, where *SS-Pz.Gr.Rgt.1*, *SS-Pz.Aufkl.-Abt.1* and elements of *SS-Pz.Rgt.1* were pushed back into the valley.

On 4 April, *Leibstandarte* troops went on the counterattack, managing to recapture the positions at Oberpiesting and Wöllersdorf and inflicting heavy losses on the enemy. The general situation, however, continued to worsen; the Soviets broke through the German positions in numerous places, threatening to get behind *I.SS-Pz.Korps* from the northwest.

On 5 April, the Soviet forces made a new penetration towards Tulln, threatening to cut off *I.SS-Pz.Korps* from *II.SS-Pz.Korps*, between Alland and the Danube. Faced with this new situation, *6.Panzerarmee* ordered the *12.SS-Pz.Div. "HJ"* to close the breach that separated it from the *2.SS-Pz.Div. "Das Reich"*. This also changed the contact with the *Leibstandarte*, which in the meantime had shifted to the line Haidhof-Weissenbach an der Triesting. *Kampfgruppe Nord*, consisting of *SS-Pz.Gr.Rgt.1*, *SS-Flak-Abt.1* and elements of *SS-Pz.Art.-Rgt.1*, had to move to Pottenstein, in order to repel the Soviet assaults to the north and west. In the days that followed, this same *Kampfgruppe* continued to fight at Pottenstein, Berndorf and Weissenbach. The SS grenadiers established their positions in a forest north of Pottenstein and, from there, threw back all of the Soviet infantry attacks, mainly at night. The division headquarters was also set up at Pottenstein.

On 6 April, the Soviets shifted their attacks mainly against the positions of *II.SS-Pz.Korps*, while in the *Leibstandarte* sector, they sought to get around Pottenstein from the north and Berndorf from the south; an attack south of Berndorf was repulsed outside of Kleinfeld, while towards Neusiedl the Soviet troops were able to make a new breakthrough between the German positions.

On 7 April, the Soviets pressed their attacks, once again encountering stiff resistance from *Leibstandarte* troops. In the area around Pottenstein, the *Panzergruppe* was able to destroy at least eleven enemy tanks. A *Kampfgruppe* consisting of elements of *SS-Pz.Gr.Rgt.1* and the *SS-Div.-Sich.-Kp.1* were engaged on Hill 475 to push back an enemy formation that had been able to approach Pottenstein from the north. But under Soviet pressure, that *Kampfgruppe* finally had to withdraw to the north of the city. Reinforcements were urgently needed in order to continue to maintain an intact defensive front; to fill the new breach between the positions of *SS-Pz.Aufkl.-Abt.1* and the *12.SS-Pz.Div.* in the Klausen-Leopoldsdorf sector, personnel from the divisional logistics train were scraped up.

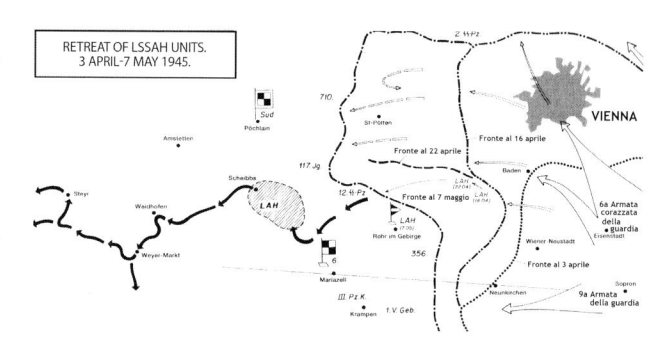

Another photo of Peiper and Martin Gross in Austria in April 1945.

A group of *Waffen SS* soldiers in a defensive position.

Also during 8 April, the Soviets continued to attack the *Leibstandarte* positions, throwing in assault groups consisting of infantry supported by tanks, mainly in the Pottenstein-Berndorf area; despite this incessant pressure, the SS troops continued to defend their positions tenaciously and to maintain their lines intact.

The last Kampfgruppen

Between 8 and 10 April, the crews without tanks and the personnel of the logistics train of *I./SS-Pz.Rgt.1* were assembled in the Rotheau-Eschenau area and were used to form an infantry combat group consisting of about 150 men. This group, placed under the command of *SS-Ustuf.* Rolf Reiser, was attached to *SS-Kampfgruppe Kling*. *SS-Ostubaf.* Peiper had in fact organized what was left of his regiment into three *Kampfgruppen*: the

One of the last photos of Peiper taken in Austria.

SS troops pulling back, in an Austrian village. Several *Panzerfaust* are on board the *Schwimmwagen*.

A group of SS soldiers, hidden in the ruins of a house destroyed by Soviet shelling.

first, *Kampfgruppe Peiper*, consisting of some Panthers and Tiger IIs, was committed to the Hainfeld-Treisen sector. *Kampfgruppe Kling*, consisting of some Tiger II tanks of *s.SS-Pz.Abt.501*, elements of infantry and other troops, was engaged in the defense of Wilhelmsburg. Finally, *Kampfgruppe Sternebeck*, consisting of the last of the Panzer IV of the *6. and 7.Kp.* was engaged in the Triesting Valley, at Fahrafeld, Weissenbach, Neuhaus and Altenmarkt.

On 9 April, with the beginning of fighting in the Vienna sector, the situation in the Pottenstein-Berndorf sector became quieter.

On 10 April, the Soviets launched a massive attack in the St. Pölten region, encircling the positions held by the *Leibstandarte*, from Neusiedl to Haidldorf. *SS-Pz.Gr.Rgt.2*, supported by several Jagdpanzer IV, managed to block an enemy penetration at Veitsau, on the hills at Pöllau. Another enemy breakthrough north of Pottenstein was blocked by *SS-Pz.Gr.Rgt.1* and by *Kampfgruppe Sternebeck*, east of Fahrafeld.

On 12 April, the Soviets resumed their attack along the Pottenstein-Hainfeld road, attempting to exploit their new breakthrough at Pöllau.

During the morning of 13 April, the *II.(gemischte) Abt.-SS-Pz.Rgt.1* under *SS-Stubaf.* Paul Guhl reached Weissenbach, coming from Rahden. The personnel of his companies, no longer with any hope of being equipped with new tanks, had been loaded aboard a train on 27 March, with orders to reach the division and to be employed as a regular infantry unit. It was Guhl's infantry-tankers who succeeded in throwing the Soviets out of Pöllau; a subsequent counterattack of theirs was halted outside of Steinhof.

On 14 April, *II.SS-Pz.Rgt.1* renewed its attack against Steinhof, with support by elements of *SS-Pz.Gr.Rgt.2*. Losses were heavy, but the battalion was able to recapture the position at Steiberg.

On 15 April, the Soviets attacked St.Pölten with two tank brigades and a mechanized brigade, continuing their offensive to the west and to the south, following the railway line. The Red Army troops were checked near Herzogenburg. Their forward elements clashed with *Kampfgruppe Kling*, in the Traisen Valley, forcing them to withdraw to the north. In the Triesting Valley, a new counterattack by *SS-Pz.Gr.Rgt.2* and by *II./SS-Pz.Gr.Rgt.1* allowed the former defensive line to be re-established, between Berndorf and Pottenstein, while the position at Steinhof was recaptured by *5.Kp./SS-Pz.Rgt.1*. In the meantime, *SS-Werfer-Abt.1* was sent to support *SS-Kampfgruppe Keitel* of the *37.SS-Kav.Div.* in the Puchberg area.

A German anti-tank squad armed with *Panzerschreck*.

Loading munitions on a *Panzerwerfer 42*.

A *Waffen SS* mortar squad.

German soldiers repelling an attack.

On 16 April, defensive fighting continued in the St.Pölten area: *Kampfgruppe Kling* had to give up the position at Georgen, succeeding however in blocking enemy forces near Wilhelmsburg. Other Soviet attacks took place against the position at Steinhof. In the *12.SS* sector, the Soviets were able to break through the defensive front at Kienberg and Gadenweith, thus managing to enter the Triesting Valley. A counterattack was quickly mounted, employing a *Kampfgruppe* of the *Leibstandarte*, consisting of elements of *SS-Pz.Gr.Rgt.1* and *Panzergruppe Sternebeck*.

On 17 April, following the relief of part of the *12.SS*, the *Leibstandarte* had to extend its defensive line as far as Neuhaus. The Soviets attacked between Weissenbach and Fahrafeld, but were repulsed by *Panzergruppe Sternebeck*. *Einsatzgruppe Peiper* was engaged in the Schöpfl area, where the Soviets attacked repeatedly and the mountain changed hands continually. All of the attacks against the positon at St.Corona were also driven back. On the other hand, a fresh attack enabled the Soviets to break into the German positions at Hegerberg; from there, the enemy forces proceeded south, bypassing the positions defended by *Einsatzgruppe Peiper* at Perschenegg. Some Soviet units turned to the east and attacked Peiper's troops from the rear. At the same time, another enemy force attacked towards Gölsenhof, engaging *Kampfgruppe Kling*; the SS troops succeeded in repelling the enemy troops who had penetrated the northern part of Wilhelmsburg, destroying at least eleven Soviet tanks.

On 18 April, the Soviets returned to attack the left flank of *I.SS-Pz.Korps* in force, in the Fahrafeld-Wald-Wilhelmsburg sector; numerous infantry units, supported by an entire tank corps, were able to break through the SS positions at Michelbach and get as far as Stollberg. A counterattack made by *Einsatzgruppe Peiper*, from the sector northwest of Hainfeld, destroyed at least fifteen enemy tanks. Other fierce

A Soviet tank column in Austria, April 1945.

A German soldier armed with a *Panzerfaust*.

A *Flakvierling* mounted on a half-track.

SS-Ostubaf. Joachim Peiper, April 1945.

clashes took place at Schwarzenbach, to the east of Wilhelmsburg, with *III.(gep.)/2* busy recapturing the city. The Soviets then circled the position from the southeast, surrounding one of the companies of the SS battalion. To free it, the SS troops had to fight bitterly, incurring heavy losses. The Soviets adopted the same tactics at Wilhelmsburg, surrounding *Kampfgruppe Kling* south of the city.

On 19 April, enemy assaults continued against the flank of *I.SS-Pz.Korps*; in the Traisen Valley, the Soviets reached as far as Rotheau, where they were stopped by *Einsatzgruppe Peiper*. Further to the east, they seized Schwarzenbach and advance towards the Gölsen Valley. The villages of St.Veit and Kropsdorf had to be abandoned before a counterattack by Peiper's men was able to free them again. Another enemy attack from the Michelbach area was stalled in the vicinity of Rohrbach by a *Kampfgruppe* of *SS-Pz.Rgt.1* and by *Panzergruppe Sternebeck*.

The following day as well, the Soviets continued their attacks southward in the St.Pölten area, again threatening the villages of St.Veit and Kropsdorf, defended by infantry troops of *Einsatzgruppe Peiper*. Other attacks were made against Rohrbach, which changed hands several times throughout the day. Thanks to the arrival of several panzers, the Soviets were pushed back further to the north. The position at Hainfeld, however, fell into enemy hands; from that position the Soviets were able to control the roads of the Triesting Valley and Gölsen. *SS-Brigdf.* Kumm ordered Hainfeld to be recaptured; *Einsatzgruppe Peiper* was to attack from the west and the *Kampfgruppe* of *SS-Pz.Gr.Rgt.2* from the east. The road could thus be reopened, but fighting inside Hainfeld continued late into the night. The Soviet infantry attacked en masse, but suffered heavy losses, mainly due to the devastating fire of a *Flakvierling*. Also on 20 April 1945, Peiper was promoted to the rank of *SS-Standartenführer*.

Rearguard actions

Also on 21 April, the Soviets exerted strong pressure against the left flank of *I.SS-Pz.Korps*. Moving from the Berndorf area, continuous attacks were made to the southwest, attempting to seize Hainfeld. Following the railway line, some enemy troops succeeded in encircling the city; Peiper threw a tank company and the *9.(pi.)Kp/SS-Pz.Rgt.1* in a counterattack, but without any success. The SS troops than had to pull back to the hills of Ödhofen. In the Wilhelmsburg sector as well, fighting resumed and also there the SS troops had to withdraw.

On 23 April, the Soviets advanced in the Triesting and Gölsen valleys; on the left of the *Leibstandarte*, the *II.SS-Pz.Rgt.1* and *SS-Pz.Gr.Rgt.2* were pushed back along the line Waxeneck-Grabenwegdörfl-Fahrafeld. The positon at Steinfeld was lost and soon after that at Grabenwegdörfl was as well. *I.SS-Pz.Korps* had to retreat further to the south. The troops were by now exhausted by the continuous fighting. a part of *Gruppe Peiper* that was between Hainfeld and Rohrbach and which had to fall back through the Halbach Valley was engaged in new clashes against superior enemy forces. The rest of *Gruppe Peiper* withdrew in the Traisen Valley, moveing to Lilienfeld. In the meantime, the division headquarters had moved to Pernitz.

During the day of 24 April, the eastern group of the *Leibstandarte* continued its withdrawal, passing through the Piesting Valley. On the right flank of the division, *Gruppe Peiper* pulled back slowly to the south, across the Halbach Valley, then to reach Kleinzell to the north. Between 25 and 26 April, defensive combat continued in the Kleinzell and Kalte Kuchl area.

Beginning on 27 April, the *Leibstandarte* troops found themselves marching in the mountains, continuing to fight against Soviet forces that were pursuing them. The objective at that point of the war, which was now lost, was to reach the American lines and avoid ending up in Soviet hands.

On 7 May 1945, following the signing of the German surrender at Reims, Otto Kumm ordered his men to cross the River Enns near Steyr, to surrender to the American forces. Most of what was left of the *Leibstandarte* was able to cross the demarcation line by the date of 9 May.

Peiper, accompanied by Paul Guhl, attempted to evade capture. On 28 May he was captured by the Americans near Schliersee, on the road to Rottach. Subjected to many trials in the post-war period and after a number of years in jail, Peiper was released in 1956. Working as a translator, he moved to Traves, in France. On 13 July 1876 he was killed in a fire in his French home, following an attack by left-wing terrorists.

German soldiers captured by the Americans, May 1945.

Soviet tanks and soldiers entering an Austrian village.

SS grenadiers aboard a tank.

Service record data (Dienstlaufbahn) for Joachim Peiper

The information in the table reflects the following data in sequence: Date (*Jahr*, *Tag* and *Monat*), rank (*Dienstgrad*), unit affiliation (*Einheit*) and function within the unit (*Art der Dienst...*).

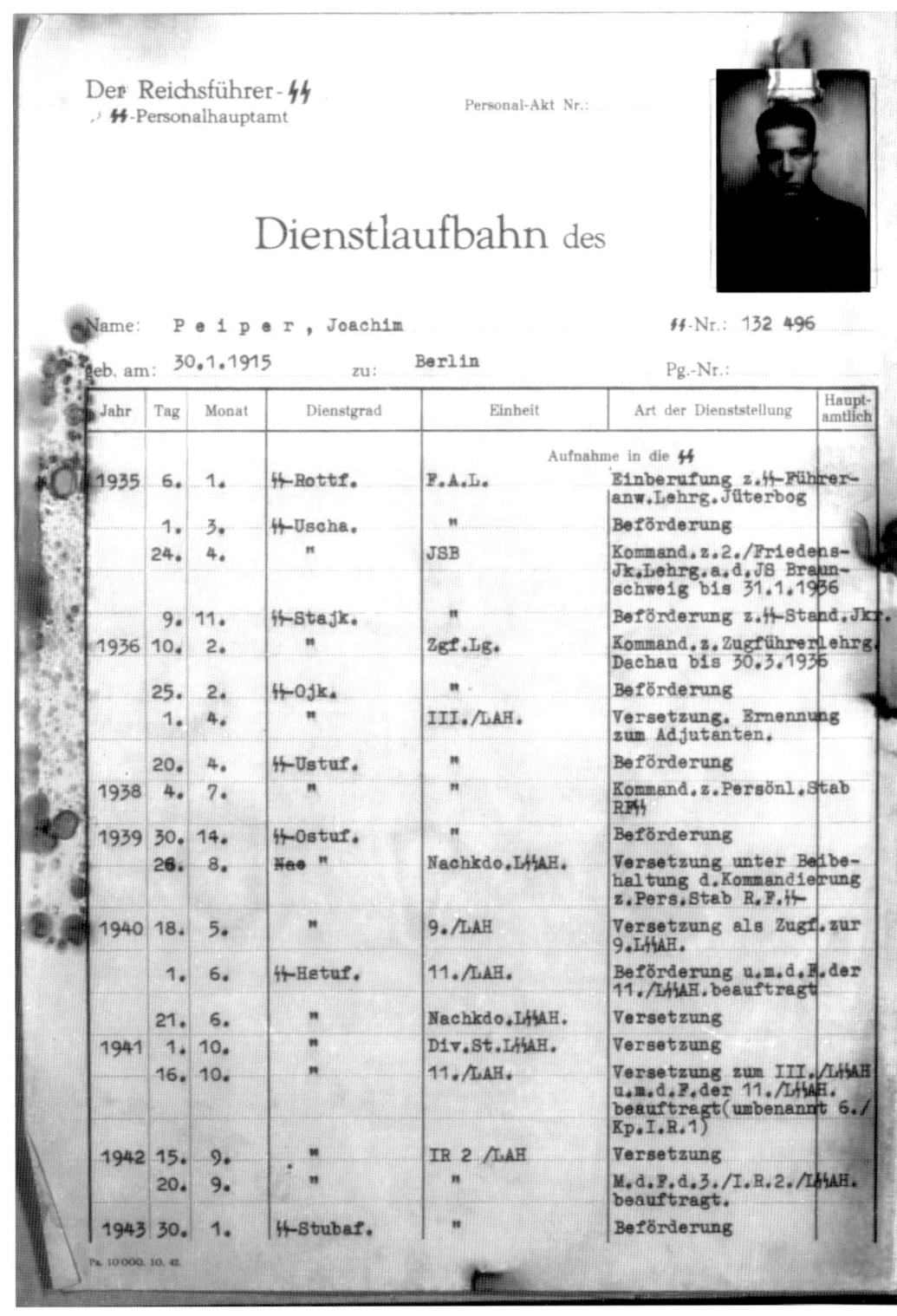

Der Reichsführer-SS
SS-Personalhauptamt

Personal-Akt Nr.:

Dienstlaufbahn des

Name: **P e i p e r , Joachim**   SS-Nr.: 132 496
geb. am: 30.1.1915   zu: Berlin   Pg.-Nr.:

Jahr	Tag	Monat	Dienstgrad	Einheit	Art der Dienststellung	Hauptamtlich
				Aufnahme in die SS		
1935	6.	1.	SS-Rottf.	F.A.L.	Einberufung z.SS-Führeranw.Lehrg.Jüterbog	
	1.	3.	SS-Uscha.	"	Beförderung	
	24.	4.	"	JSB	Kommand.z.2./Friedens-Jk.Lehrg.a.d.JS Braunschweig bis 31.1.1936	
	9.	11.	SS-Stajk.	"	Beförderung z.SS-Stand.Jkr.	
1936	10.	2.	"	Zgf.Lg.	Kommand.z.Zugführerlehrg. Dachau bis 30.3.1936	
	25.	2.	SS-Ojk.	"	Beförderung	
	1.	4.	"	III./LAH.	Versetzung. Ernennung zum Adjutanten.	
	20.	4.	SS-Ustuf.	"	Beförderung	
1938	4.	7.	"	"	Kommand.z.Persönl.Stab RFSS	
1939	30.	14.	SS-Ostuf.	"	Beförderung	
	26.	8.	"	Nachkdo.LSSAH.	Versetzung unter Beibehaltung d.Kommandierung z.Pers.Stab R.F.SS	
1940	18.	5.	"	9./LAH	Versetzung als Zugf. zur 9.LSSAH.	
	1.	6.	SS-Hstuf.	11./LAH.	Beförderung u.m.d.F.der 11./LSSAH.beauftragt	
	21.	6.	"	Nachkdo.LSSAH.	Versetzung	
1941	1.	10.	"	Div.St.LSSAH.	Versetzung	
	16.	10.	"	11./LAH.	Versetzung zum III./LSSAH u.m.d.F.der 11./LSSAH. beauftragt(umbenannt 6./Kp.I.R.1)	
1942	15.	9.	"	IR 2 /LAH	Versetzung	
	20.	9.	"	"	M.d.F.d.3./I.R.2./LSSAH. beauftragt.	
1943	30.	1.	SS-Stubaf.	"	Beförderung	

The document is only current until 1943. (Berlin Document Center).

List of awards and promotions

Document from 1944, with functions and awards. (BDC)

SS-Obsrsturmführer Joachim Peiper.

Peiper's Promotions

Rank	Date
SS-Anwärter	16 October 1933
SS-Mann	23 January 1934
SS-Sturmmann	7 September 1934
SS-Rottenführer	10 October 1934
SS-Unterscharführer	1 March 1935
SS-Standartenjunker	11 September 1935
SS-Standartenoberjunker	5 March 1936
SS-Untersturmführer	20 April 1936
SS-Obersturmführer	30 January 1939
SS-Hauptsturmführer	6 June 1940
SS-Sturmbannführer	30 January 1943
SS-Obersturmbannführer	11 November 1943
SS-Standartenführer	20 April 1945

Metz, September 1940: Himmler and Peiper.

Geographical terminology

Award	Date
Iron Cross Second Class	31 May 1940
Iron Cross First Class	1 June 1940
Assault Infantry Badge in Bronze	July 1940
Eastern Front Medal (Ostfrontmedaille)	August 1942
Knight's Cross	9 March 1943
German Cross in Gold	6 May 1943
Tank Killer Badge	21 July 1943
Close-quarter Combat Badge in Bronze	7 September 1943
Close-quarter Combat Badge in Silver	20 October 1943
Oak Leaves	27 January 1944
Swords	11 January 1945
Wound Badge in Black	-
Tank Assault Badge in Silver	-
Tank Assault Badge in Silver for 25 actions	-

Peiper, winter 1941-42

SS-Stubaf. Joachim Peiper in a 1943 photo, with the Knight's Cross.

Two photos of Peiper in France, 1940.

Bibliography

Primary sources

Public archives
Bundesarchiv Berlin, Lichterfelde, Germany
Bundesarchiv-Militärarchiv Freiburg, Germany
U.S. National Archives, Washington D.C., USA
Vojensky Historicky Archiv Praga, Czech Republic

Period magazines and publications
Signal magazine, various editions and issues
Das Schwarze Korps magazine, various issues

Secondary sources: published books

M. Afiero. *Leibstandarte SS Adolf Hitler, 1933-1943.* Associazione Culturale Ritterkreuz

M. Afiero. *Leibstandarte SS Adolf Hitler, 1943-1945.* Associazione Culturale Ritterkreuz

P. Agte. *Jochen Peiper, Kommandeur Panzerregiment Leibstandarte.* Kurt Vowinckel Verlag, 1998

T. Fischer. *Das Panzer-Artillerie-Regiment 1 LAH an allen Fronten 1940-1945.* Podzun-Pallas Verlag, 200.

T. Fischer. *Von Berlin bis Caen. Entwicklung und Einsätze der Divisions-und-Korps-Artillerie der LAH.* Helios Verlag, 2004

R. Lehmann. *Die Leibstandarte: vol 1-3.* Munin Verlag, Osnabrück, 1977-1982

R. Lehmann, R. Tiemann. *Die Leibstandarte: vol IV/1-2.* Munin Verlag, Osnabrück, 1986

R. Lehmann. *Die Leibstandarte: vol im Bild.* Munin Verlag, Osnabrück, 1983

G. Nipe, R. Spezzano. *Platz der Leibstandarte.* RZM Publishing, 2002

R. Tiemann. *Chronicle of the 7.Panzer-Kompanie 1.SS-Panzer-Division „LSSAH".* Schiffer Publishing, 1998

C. Trang. *Liebstandarte 1933-1942.* Editions Heimdal

C. Trang. *Liebstandarte 1943-1945.* Editions Heimdal

H. Walther. *Die 1.SS-Panzerdivision.* Podzun-Pallas Verlag, 1987

J. Weingartner. *Hitler's Guard: The Story of the Leibstandarte SS Adolf Hitler, 1933-1945.* South Ill. Univ. Press

J. Westmeier. *Joachim Peiper. A Biography of Himmler's SS Commander.* Schiffer Publishing

Periodical publications
Der Freiwillige magazine, various issues
Siegrunen magazine, periodical published by Richard Landwehr, several issues
Ritterkreuz, bimonthly publication dedicated to Waffen SS formations, several issues

Painted by Jacek Pasieczny

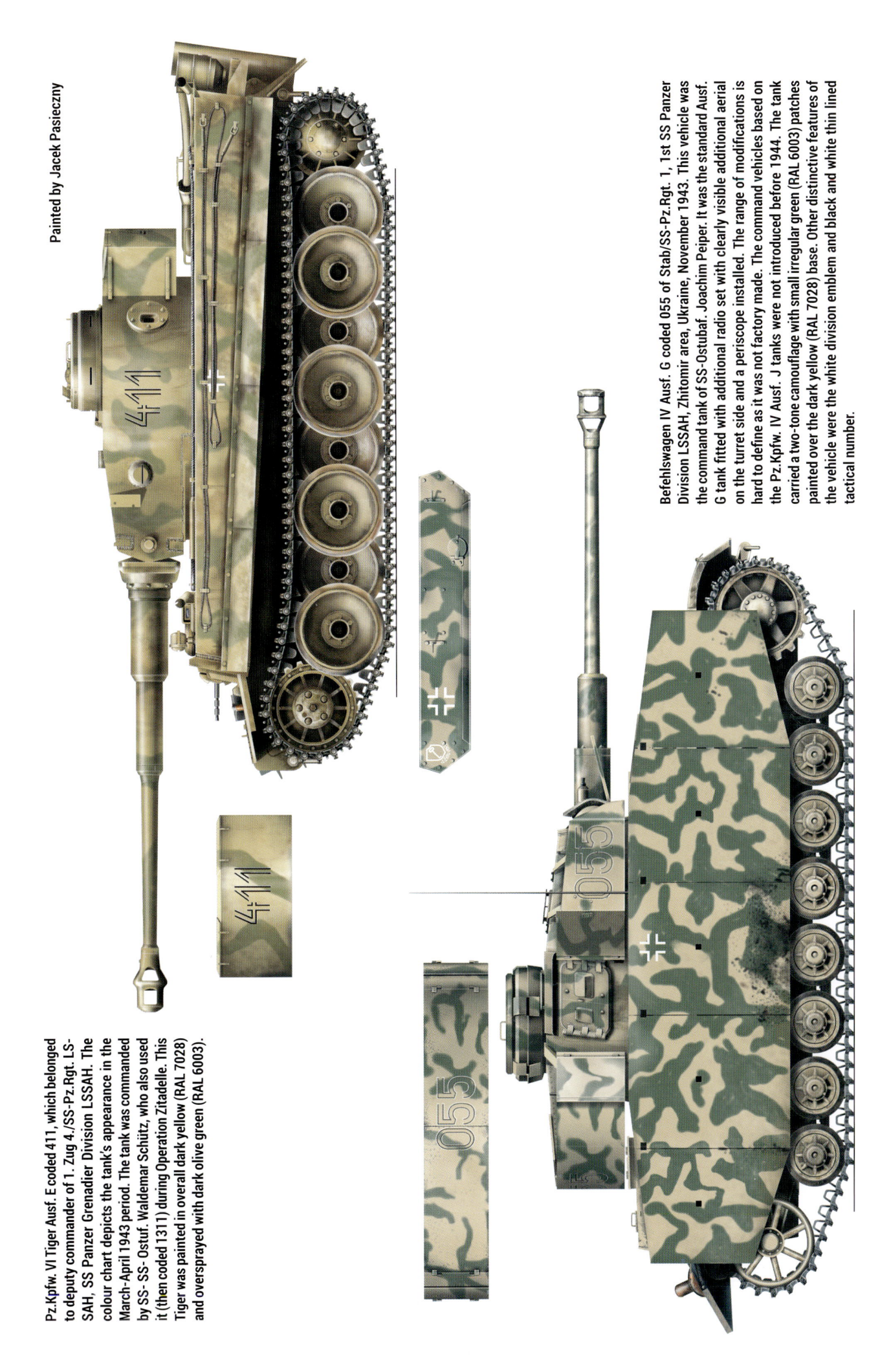

Pz.Kpfw. VI Tiger Ausf. E coded 411, which belonged to deputy commander of 1. Zug 4./SS-Pz.Rgt. LSSAH, SS Panzer Grenadier Division LSSAH. The colour chart depicts the tank's appearance in the March-April 1943 period. The tank was commanded by SS- SS- Ostuf. Waldemar Schütz, who also used it (then coded 1311) during Operation Zitadelle. This Tiger was painted in overall dark yellow (RAL 7028) and oversprayed with dark olive green (RAL 6003).

Befehlswagen IV Ausf. G coded 055 of Stab/SS-Pz.Rgt. 1, 1st SS Panzer Division LSSAH, Zhitomir area, Ukraine, November 1943. This vehicle was the command tank of SS-Ostubaf. Joachim Peiper. It was the standard Ausf. G tank fitted with additional radio set with clearly visible additional aerial on the turret side and a periscope installed. The range of modifications is hard to define as it was not factory made. The command vehicles based on the Pz.Kpfw. IV Ausf. J tanks were not introduced before 1944. The tank carried a two-tone camouflage with small irregular green (RAL 6003) patches painted over the dark yellow (RAL 7028) base. Other distinctive features of the vehicle were the white division emblem and black and white thin lined tactical number.

Painted by Jacek Pasieczny

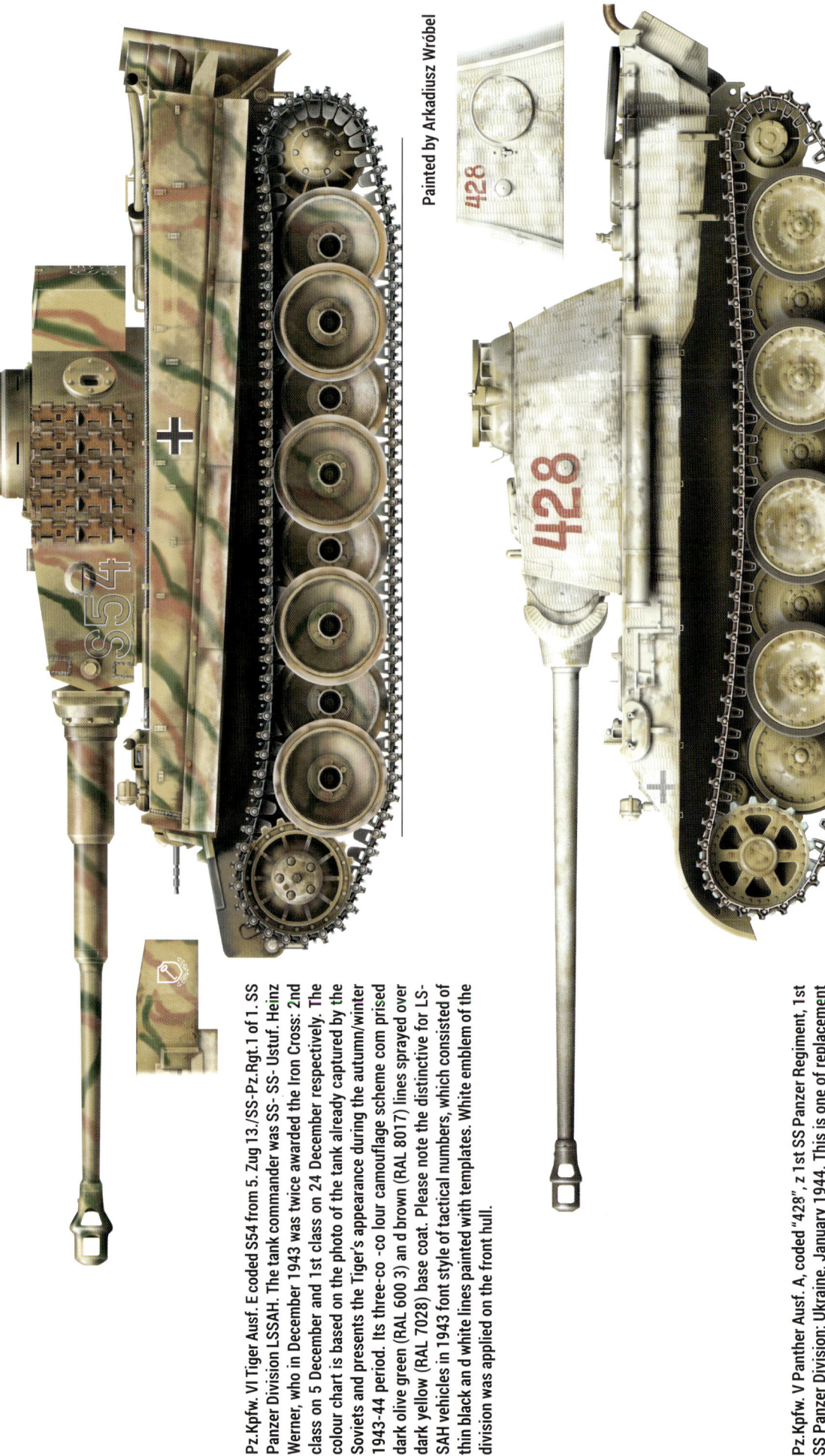

Painted by Arkadiusz Wróbel

Pz.Kpfw. VI Tiger Ausf. E coded S54 from 5. Zug 13./SS-Pz.Rgt.1 of 1. SS Panzer Division LSSAH. The tank commander was SS- SS- Ustuf. Heinz Werner, who in December 1943 was twice awarded the Iron Cross: 2nd class on 5 December and 1st class on 24 December respectively. The colour chart is based on the photo of the tank already captured by the Soviets and presents the Tiger's appearance during the autumn/winter 1943-44 period. Its three-co -co lour camouflage scheme com prised dark olive green (RAL 600 3) an d brown (RAL 8017) lines sprayed over dark yellow (RAL 7028) base coat. Please note the distinctive for LS-SAH vehicles in 1943 font style of tactical numbers, which consisted of thin black and white lines painted with templates. White emblem of the division was applied on the front hull.

Pz.Kpfw. V Panther Ausf. A, coded "428", z 1st SS Panzer Regiment, 1st SS Panzer Division; Ukraine, January 1944. This is one of replacement tanks delivered to the unit in late December. White distemper covers dark yellow base color.

110

Painted by Arkadiusz Wróbel

Pz.Kpfw. V Panther Ausf. G, coded "131", of the 1st SS Panzer Regiment, 1st SS Panzer Division; the Ardennes, December 1944. At that time only the 1st and 2nd companies were armed with this type of tank. Overall, on 3rd December 1944 there were 42 Panthers on strength in the 1st SS Panzer Regiment. This tank was knocked out on 18th December near Cheneux. Of interest is the turret camouflage which comprised olive green and red brown dots.

Late production series Jagdpanzer IV L/70 (V) belonging to SS-Panzerjäger-Abteilung 1 of 1. SS Armoured Division Liebstandarte Adolf Hitler, supporting Kampfgruppe Hansen. The vehicle has the Hiterhalt-Tarnung camouflage scheme. Poteau region (Ardennes), December 1944.